'Saving' Education

Higher Education Leadership & Study of Historically Black Colleges and Universities

Series Editor
Hakim J. Lucas
Virginia Union University, USA

The series in Higher Education Leadership and Study of Historically Black Colleges and Universities aim at disseminating knowledge about the continuity between the leadership practices in Higher Educational management of historically Black Colleges and Universities. The series show that managing historically Black colleges and universities requires, on one hand, abiding by the mission of the founding fathers of these institutions and requires a unique style of leadership, while striving to educate students to compete and meet the demands of the 21st century labor market

OTHER TITLES IN THE HIGHER EDUCATION LEADERSHIP & STUDY OF HISTORICALLY BLACK COLLEGES AND UNIVERSITIES SERIES

Modern Heroics: How HBCUs Navigated the COVID-19 Pandemic (2022)
Hakim J. Lucas, Herman J. Felton. ISBN 978-1-64802-973-8

Not for Ourselves Alone: The Legacies of Two Pioneers of Black Higher Education in the United States (2019)
Hakim J. Lucas. ISBN 978-1-64113-789-8

'Saving' Education

Religion and/in Historically Black Colleges and Universities

Edited by

Anthony B. Pinn

Rice University, USA

emerald
PUBLISHING

United Kingdom – North America – Japan
India – Malaysia – China

Emerald Publishing Limited
Emerald Publishing, Floor 5, Northspring, 21-23 Wellington Street, Leeds LS1 4DL

First edition 2025

Cover photo: iStock

Reprints and permissions service
Contact: www.copyright.com

British Library Cataloguing in Publication Data
A catalogue record for this book is available from the British Library

ISBN: 978-1-83708-895-9 (Print hardback)
ISBN: 978-1-83708-897-3 (Print paperback)
ISBN: 978-1-83708-894-2 and 978-1-83708-896-6 (Ebook)

Typeset by TNQ Tech
Cover design by TNQ Tech

CONTENTS

ABOUT THE EDITOR

Anthony B. Pinn is currently the Agnes Cullen Arnold Distinguished Professor of Humanities and professor of religion at Rice University. He is also Professor Extraordinarius at the University of South Africa. In addition, Pinn is a fellow of the American Academy of Arts and Sciences. Pinn is the founding director of the Center for Engaged Research and Collaborative Learning, and he served as the inaugural director of the Center for African and African American Studies both at Rice University. He is managing editor of *Religious Studies Review*. Pinn's research interests include African American religious thought, religion and culture; humanism; and hip hop culture. Pinn is co-editor of numerous book series, including (with Stacey Floyd-Thomas) "Religion and Social Transformation" (NYU Press) and (with Monica Miller) "Routledge Studies in Religion and Hip Hop" (Routledge). He also serves on the board of several journals, including the *Journal of Religion*, the *Journal of Africana Religion*, and the journal *Body and Religion*. He is the author/editor of over 35 books, including *The Interplay of Things: Religion, Art, and Presence Together* (Duke, 2021) and the novel *The New Disciples* (2015).

ABOUT THE CONTRIBUTORS

Cecil Andrew Duffie serves as the Dean of the Julius S. Scott, Sr. Chapel of Wiley College in Marshall, Texas. As one of the youngest executive officers of collegiate religious and spiritual life, Dr. Duffie is widely known for his obsession with the marriage of education and faith, enthusiasm for Black religious history, and excitement for college and university chaplaincy. Dr. Duffie earned a Ph.D., M.Div., and a Certificate of Executive Leadership with distinction from Howard University. He also holds a B.S. in Telecommunication with a minor in Education from the University of Florida. He became a licensed minister in 2012 and was ordained in 2017. Dr. Duffie's research, which has been presented at Yale University, Trinity College, Howard University, and other institutions, is centered around spiritual formation, and college and university Black chaplaincy in the 21st century. His honors and awards include: Florida Blue Key; University of Florida Outstanding Leader; Alpha Phi Alpha Region & District College Brother of the Year; the Evans Crawford Graduate Assistantship; the Howard University Trustee Scholarship; the Ivan Earle Taylor Scholarship; and the Joseph H. Jackson Scholarship.

Karen Kossie-Chernyshev, a fifth generation Texas and native Houstonian, is three times a graduate of Rice University and the first African American to earn a Ph.D. in History from a Texas institution. She also holds an M.A. in Francophone African Literature from Michigan State University. She has hosted local and international workshops and published scholarly essays and chapters on African American history and religion with the support of numerous fellowships and grants, including awards from the National Endowment for the Humanities, Humanities Texas (Texas Council for the Humanities), Summerlee Foundation, and the Mickey Leland Center for World Peace (Texas Southern University). Her edited works include *Angie Brown: A Jim Crow Romance* (Outskirts Press, 2017) and *Recovering Five Generations Hence: The Life and Writing of Lillian Jones Horace* (Texas A & M University Press, 2013), which showcases selected overlook works by Texas's earliest known African American woman novelist, Lillian Jones Horace (1880–1965). Dr. Kossie-Chernyshev is currently working on a digital, multi-media project on Horace's life and works thanks in part to her participation in "Born Digital Scholarly Publishing," an NEH Seminar hosted by Brown University (2022).

Hakim J. Lucas serves as President & Chief Executive Officer at Virginia Union University. He has nearly two decades of progressive leadership experience in higher education. His career successes include fundrais-ing, strategic planning, and the engagement and retention of students at Historically Black Colleges and Universities. In addition, he sits on several boards including Partnership for Families, Southern Education Founda-tion, Venture Richmond, and the SunTrust Advisory Council. Dr. Lucas earned a bachelor's degree from Morehouse College, a master's degree in education from Tufts University, an Executive MBA from Stetson University, and a Master of Divinity from Union Theological Seminary. He earned his doctoral degree in education from Fordham University. He is active with several advisory councils and organizations including Alpha Phi Alpha Fra-ternity, Inc., Prince Hall Free Masonry, and 100 Black Men. Dr. Lucas is a senior research fellow with the Southern Education Foundation. In 2019, his latest book was published titled *Not For Ourselves Alone: Legacies of Two Pioneers of Black Higher Education in the United States*.

Melanye Price is a Special Assistant to the President of Prairie View A&M University and inaugural director of The Ruth J. Simmons Center for Race and Justice. Price holds an Endowed Professorship in Political Science and served as the principal investigator for their African American Studies Ini-tiative, which is funded by the Mellon Foundation. Price is the author of two books: *The Race Whisperer: Barack Obama and the Political Uses of Race* (NYU) and *Dreaming Blackness: Black Nationalism and African American Public Opinion* (NYU). She completed her B.A. magna cum laude in geography at Prairie View A&M University and her M.A. and Ph.D. in political science at The Ohio State University. Price was the 2017 Black History Month lecturer for the US Embassy in Germany where she lectured at universities and com-munity organizations across the country. She is a regular contributor for the *New York Times* Opinion section and has also done political commentary for MSNBC, CNN, *Ms. Magazine*, *Elle Magazine* and National Public Radio.

Quincy James Rineheart is an African American religious historian, Rustin-ian scholar, theologian, academic activist, and teacher. He is a Doctor of Philosophy Candidate at the Chicago Theological Seminary. He is writing a dissertation entitled "Recovering Bayard Rustin: The Black Quaker Spiri-tuality of a Civil Rights Architect." Recently, he received the Dissertation

Fellowship for the Forum for Theological Exploration. He specializes in African American historiography, Black Religious History, Black Queer Theory, Gender & Sexuality Studies, and Black Masculinity and Cultural Studies. He earned a Bachelor of Arts in Literature (*cum laude*) from Wilberforce University; a Master of Divinity in Ethics and Theology with a certificate in Black Church Studies from Emory University; and a Master of Sacred Theology in Theological Studies from Chicago Theological Seminary. In addition to his academic and administrative responsibilities, he serves as a member of the Chicago Black Gay Men's Caucus Board of Directors. Rineheart served as the Associate Campus Minister and Adjunct Professor of Africana Studies at Morehouse College, and he is now Executive Assistant to the President and Assistant Director of the Anderson Ecumenical Institute at Payne Theological Seminary.

Cleve V. Tinsley IV is an Assistant Professor of History and Political Science in the School of Arts and Sciences at Virginia Union University (VUU), where he has also been appointed the inaugural Executive Director of the Center for African-American History and Culture (CAAHC). Trained as a critical theorist of religion and Black culture, he employs interdisciplinary research—informed by humanistic theoretical approaches and methods in the social sciences—to interpret the religious significance and meaning of various African-American formations, freedom struggles, and cultural productions. Tinsley is quickly emerging as a noted interpreter of religion and Black freedom struggles, recently commenting on the role of religion in light of recent uprisings for Black lives for the Berkley Center for Religion, Peace and World Affairs at Georgetown University. He is the co-author of *Embodiment and Black Religion: Rethinking the Body in African-American Religious Experience* (Equinox Publishing) and is working on his first monograph, tentatively entitled *Making Black Lives Matter: Religion and Race in the Struggle for African-American Identity*.

FOREWORD

Blest Be This Tie: Historically Black Colleges
and Universities and the Black Church.
Hakim J. Lucas

The African American Heritage Hymnal #341 reflects the thoughts of John Fawcett, orphan tailor preacher born in 1782 and converted in a methodist revival. Fawcett pens words that have been orphaned, tailored and preached by African American religious and education leaders for over 200 years:

> Blest be the tie that binds our hearts in Christian love; the fellowship of kindred minds is like to that above. Before our Father's throne we pour our ardent prayers; our fears, our hopes, our aims are one, our comfort and our cares. We share our mutual woes, our mutual burdens bear, and often for each other flow the sympathizing tear. (1987)

Mindful of these words, I propose that the historically Black college and university (HBCU) and the Black Church (Church) are organizational siblings. Fraternal twins, they were born within seconds of each other. Birthed to their parents, Black justice and Black empowerment in the cradle of American slavery and injustice. The HBCU and Church have an interesting history together and apart. Oftentimes hard to distinguish, these anchors of African experience in the United States have guided the maturation of Black people who have wrestled with the multiple continuous macro- and micro-aggressions of systemic white racist oppression. Courageously, these institutions have found comfort one to the other. This comfort, though tempered by the social, political, economic and ethical turbulences of the day, has and continues to force an evolution in mission, focus, ideology and practice.

The HBCU and Church connection is identified in their meaning-making power. This shared power is the ability to provide a lens and platform for pulling on the binding tie—freedom. Freedom in its simplest form: to write, wrestle, inquire, critique, reimagine and empower. The impact of the Black Church on HBCUs is profound, shaping their founding principles, educational mission, community engagement, leadership development, cultural expression, and social activism. While some aspects have evolved, the legacy of a wonder working power that binds the continued pursuit of freedom continues to be a significant part of the identity and mission of many HBCUs.

This book is a collection of essays that, in the tradition of HBCUs and the Black Church, pull on the binding ties of the African American's maturing conceptualization and living of freedom. I believe it offers readers a good sense of some of the major issues and opportunities related to the intersections of religion and HBCUs. There is much to gain by reading these essays. And, as you read, please know that this volume in the Series is dedicated to ancestral, present and future warriors of the HBCU and Black Church family—blest be this tie!

ACKNOWLEDGMENTS

This book would not exist without the hard work of the staff of the Center for Engaged Research and Collaborative Learning (CERCL). In particular, Maya Reine—the Associate Director of the Center—not only worked out the logistics for the conference related to this project, but she also prepared the book files for submission. In addition, Hassan Henderson-Lott, my graduate student, played an important role in working through the logistics for the conference. Thank you both! Of course, a huge thank you to my colleagues who contributed to this volume. In addition, I must thank President Reginald DesRoches (Rice University) and President Hakim Lucas (Virginia Union University) for their support of the partnership between CERCL and the Center for the Study of HBCUs at Virginia Union University that guides this book and others to come. Finally, I want to express my appreciation for Suad Kamardeen, Poppy Pearce and everyone else at Emerald Publishing for moving this book from a set of files to this published product.

INTRODUCTION: CONNECTING RELIGION AND EDUCATION

Anthony B. Pinn
Rice University, USA

ABSTRACT

After offering context for the volume, the author examines briefly the emergence of historically Black colleges and universities (HBCUs) within the historical context of white supremacy and racial trauma. Related to this, the author argues that HBCUs played a significant role in not only offering academic opportunity but also nurtured a population of African Americans who understood themselves as obligated to the betterment of their community. In a word, HBCUs have been vital with respect to the advance of African Americans. Furthermore, the author gives attention to the manner in which the work of these HBCUs is tied to religious organizations in that denominational support was vital during their initial development. But more than a financial tie, the author notes that HBCUs also often draw their moral and ethical sensibilities from religious communities—thereby tying educational advancement to the full well-being of the larger African American community. Finally, the author summarizes the various chapters in light of this connection and with respect to a range of questions guiding the book—e.g., How do some of the significant figures formed within associated socio-cultural, intellectual, and theological environments define these educational communities and their mission(s)?

Keywords: Black religion; Reconstruction; vision; mission; philanthropists; pedagogy

'Saving' Education, pages 1–6
Copyright © 2025 by Emerald Publishing Limited
doi:10.1108/978-1-83708-894-220251001

These conference proceedings stem from an effort to rethink the nature of interaction between predominantly white institutions and historically Black colleges and universities (HBCUs). Beginning with Rice University and Virginia Union University, the goal has been to amplify areas of shared interest while also recognizing differences. For some, this work might seem obvious, a longstanding exchange; however, is that really the case? And, to the degree there are such connections, have they been maximized?

There is need still for imaginative and creative transformations of higher education—guided by a central aim of fostering academic leadership with the capacity, skills, and vision necessary to address the challenges of anti-Black racism and other modes of injustice infecting our society and its institutions. And, it is useful to move beyond such effort siloed on individual campuses and to engage instead in ways that serve to bridge the communicative divide between historically Black institutions of higher education and predominantly white institutions of higher education.

The partnership between Rice University and Virginia Union University in the form of a new program—Black Leadership Across Campuses (BLAC)—is meant as an intervention related to this much needed work. It serves as a pilot initiative with the potential to grow to include an expansive array of national partners.[1] To be sure, the claim isn't that Rice University and Virginia Union University have invented a unique process of collaboration, but rather that such collaboration has great potential particularly in this historical moment—with its challenges to critical thinking and the presentation of accurate history marked by the continuation of anti-Black racism. BLAC supports its mission through careful and creative attention to and implementations of a set of goals, including conferences meant to generate publications addressing key issues.

During the Fall of 2022, BLAC sponsored its first conference composed of a group of scholar-teachers and administrators exploring dimensions of a central theme: "Religion and HBCUs: History, Mission, and Impact." In extending the invitation to potential participants, the focus wasn't their personal relationship to HBCUs in an affective sense, but rather the manner in which their professional work speaks to the general theme. And, the theme was somewhat vague in order to allow for wide-ranging conversation.

CONTEXTUAL CONSIDERATIONS

Prior to the emergence of HBCUs educational attainment for African Americans had to involve informal processes that, if discovered, could result in physical threat, harm, or death. The general logic of white supremacy and white privilege in the United States reasoned that educated African Americans were *dangerous* African Americans, who would not be content to maintain a subordinate socio-economic and political position. And, this logic was to be enforced through violence when more moderate approaches failed. The Civil War and Reconstruction altered the practices of public and private life to some degree with an increase in the number of institutions of higher learning meant for African Americans. At least in theory, the end of formal slavery meant opportunity for education that would result in a range of advancements meant to represent inclusion in a "revised" national narrative. Of course, segregated life arrangements remained in place. Reconstruction failed to establish new structures for socio-political and economic arrangements in the South (and North for that matter). And, with the removal of union troops there was limited attention to the safety and general well-being of African Americans as they worked to establish themselves in light of the rhetoric of change. Still, even in this context of new modes of dehumanization and ostracization, schools developed.

Beginning with Cheyney University of Pennsylvania (1837), HBCUs existed to provide educational advancement (and its larger benefits) in a country that denied African Americans access to white institutions of higher learning. And, from that beginning to the present, there has been no doubt that HBCUs have played a major role—one beyond their resource base—in the educational and general advancement of African Americans (and over the years a large number of non-African American students and faculty). Although these institutions of higher learning make-up less than five percent of colleges and universities in the United States (roughly 100 institutions in roughly 20 states), they produce roughly twenty percent of all African American college graduates.[2] The numbers are even more impressive when one considers particular professions. For example, according to the National Science Foundation, "of the top eight institutions that graduate Black undergraduate students who ultimately go on to earn doctorates, seven are HBCUs—one-third of all Black students who have earned doctorates graduated with bachelor's degrees from HBCUs."[3] Of course, such success isn't limited to Science, Technology, Engineering and Mathematics (STEM) in that HBCU graduates who have transformed socio-cultural, political and economic life based on their training in the Humanities and Social Sciences constitute yet another impressive list.

The development of institutions like Cheyney University afforded a space in which to experiment with new ideas of life, new visions for inclusion and opportunity, and a deeper sense of one's place in the history (and future) of civilization. To think through the socio-political context for these institutions, I turn to W. E. B. Du Bois. A product of an HBCU, his written reflections on these schools (combined with having taught at several of them) offers keen insights still relevant.[4] For example, reflecting on the brutalization of Black life, Du Bois, in 1933, speaks to the ongoing nature and meaning of the HBCU when saying,

We have no assurance this twentieth century civilization will survive. We do not know that American Negroes will survive. There are sinister signs about us, antecedent to and unconnected with the Great Depression. The organized might of industry North and South is relegating the Negro to the edge of survival and using him as a labor reservoir on starvation wage. No secure professional class, no science, literature, nor art can live on such a subsoil. It is an insistent, deep-throated cry for rescue, guidance, and organized advance that greets the black leader today, and the college that rains him has got to let him know at least as much about the great black miners' strike in Alabama as about the age of Pericles.[5]

The gendered language used by Du Bois falters and doesn't capture the extent of the dilemma, one that requires the full participation of all those educated within the walls of HBCUs. For example, keep in mind that long before Du Bois wrote the words above, Mary McLeod Bethune founded the Daytona Literary and Industrial Training Institute for Negro Girls (1904), which, through a merger, would eventually become Bethune-Cookman University, with this as its mission: "...to educate a diverse community of learners to become responsible, productive citizens and solution seekers through the promotion of faith, scholarship, creative endeavors, leadership and service." The linkage between faith (in this case Black Christianity) and advancement is explicit with Mary McLeod Bethune, who argued for religiosity as grounding for all her school's efforts. This connection is evident in both her personal thinking and her theory of education. In a letter written in 1946 to Josephine T. Washington, she said,

...my philosophy of education is the basic principle upon which my life has been built—that is the three-fold training of head, hand, heart. I believe in a rounded education with a belief in the dignity and refinement of labor—in doing well whatever task is assigned to me. A belief in a spiritual undergirting [sic] of all my efforts and a clear, sane mental development.[6]

Mary McLeod Bethune reminds that there is something in the stories of HBCUs suggesting a transformative ethos that entails more than a call for material success. It also encourages a deeper growth that targets something beyond the physical. One might think of this growth as related to the "soul"—the genius—of African Americans made famous by Du Bois.[7] What he says with respect to Atlanta University could be used to frame in general terms of university praxis the inner impulse I'm trying to capture:

Not only is Atlanta University a school and a home; it is in the large sense of the word, a church. I do not mean by that anything narrow or sectarian...As the larger home, then, of its sons and Daughters, Atlanta University, is, and always has been, a teacher of religion and morality.[8]

In this way, these universities and colleges combined intellectual rigor with moral growth and ethical strength. Whether education was thought of as "classical" training, or more technical and industrial, opportunity for intellectual and practical advancement informed a sense of personhood, and of collective meaning and purpose.

Granted, not all HBCUs were founded explicitly by churches and other religious organizations. For example, there were also state and federal development institutions (e.g., Texas Southern University and Florida A&M University) as well as those organized by various philanthropists. Still, the question of religion's relationship to the mission and meaning of these institutions is worth attention. Some dimensions of the religious orientation, or ethos, of HBCUs is obvious—e.g., founded by churches, religious services as a dimension of campus community engagement, ministerial advocates. Related to this, one might think of Atlanta Baptist Female Seminary (housed in Friendship Baptist Church) founded by Sophia Packard and Harriet Giles in 1881, with the named changed to Spelman College in 1924. It was financed in part by the American Baptist Home Mission Society and John D. Rockefeller. Augusta Institute, which would become Morehouse College also was started in a church basement (1867) by three ministers, and with support from Henry Lyman Morehouse of the American Baptist Home mission Society.

Perhaps there were ways in which the religious inclinations of many of the sponsoring institutions and individuals also meant attention to filtering this educational vision—these new patterns of thought and practice—through a theological lens that framed history as teleological in nature and the advancement of African Americans as God's promise being fulfilled. The material presence of these institutions also spoke a word concerning the undergirding theology meant to link intellectual development and moral-ethical correctness. What impact did theological concerns and changes resulting from the promise and pain of Reconstruction and Jim/Jane Crow have on the ethos of these institutions and the posture toward the world of their students? How do some of the significant figures formed within associated socio-cultural, intellectual, and theological environments define these educational communities and their mission(s)? What are some of the dynamics of critical thinking needed within a predominately Black educational context, and how does critical thinking and socio-cultural critique impact pedagogy? What influence does the university or college chapel have on the nature of HBCUs and their presence in the world?

While not necessarily explicit in the following essays, such questions and the considerations they prompt do inform this slim volume composed of five essays. In fact, the above questions shadow a more general query undergirding the conference and these pieces: In relationship to this complex connection to religion, how might one describe the history, mission, and impact of HBCUs?

Taken as a whole, these essays explore both the personal and communal dimensions of the general theme, and offer insights and challenges across a range of concerns related to the various responsibilities assumed by HBCUs—particularly in light of their connection to religious thought and practice. Read together they offer a layered and multidisciplinary examination of the impact of religion on the mission and activities of HBCUs expressed over the course of centuries. It is my hope these essays that sparked rich conversation during our conference will also generate productive questions and considerations for readers.

NOTES

1. For more information on BLAC, go to the Rice University's Center for Engaged Research and Collaborative Learning Website: https://www.cercl.rice.edu/black-leadership-across-campuses.
2. https://uncf.org/the-latest/the-numbers-dont-lie-hbcus-are-changing-the-college-landscape#:~:text=Though%20HBCUs%20make%20up%20only,financial%20obstacles%20Black%20students%20face
3. https://www.nsf.gov/news/special_reports/announcements/081920.jsp
4. This would include *The Souls of Black Folk* (New York: Library of America, 1990), but his relevant work isn't limited to this text.
   In mentioning DuBois, readers shouldn't assume a rejection of advocates for more technical education, like Booker T. Washington; instead, I'm simply offering one of many possible examples of how HBCUs were viewed during their key decades of development—in relationship to religious organizations and in light of the pressing (and often deadly) consequences of anti-Black racism.
5. W. E. B. Du Bois, "The Negro College", *The Crisis* (1933, August) [Reprinted in David Leering Lewis, ed., *W. E. B. Du Bois: A Reader* (New York: Henry Holt and Company, 1995): 72–73].
6. https://www.cookman.edu/history/our-founder.html
7. See W. E. B. Du Bois, *The Souls of Black Folk* (New York: The Library of America, 1990). While the meaning of "souls" is located throughout the text, readers should pay special attention to the first chapter—"Of Our Spiritual Strivings", pp. 7–15.
8. W. E. B. Du Bois, "Atlanta University", in *From Servitude to Service: Being the Old South Lectures on the History and Work of Southern Institutions for the Education of the Negro* (Boston, MA: American Unitarian Association, 1905) [Reprinted in David Leering Lewis, ed., *W. E. B. Du Bois: A Reader* (New York: Henry Holt and Company, 1995): 248].

CHAPTER 1

TRIANGULAR TRADE TO PRODUCTIVE EXCHANGE: 150 YEARS OF BLACK CHURCH/ HBCU COLLABORATION IN TEXAS

Karen Kossie-Chernyshev
Texas Southern University, USA

ABSTRACT

This essay provides a historical description of the synergy between Black churches and historically Black colleges and universities. In so doing the author highlights Texas by discussing the manner in which its Black Baptist churches helped to foster both higher education and more general socio-economic and political well-being. For example, by exploring the relationship between Mt. Gilead Baptist Church and Prairie View A&M University, the author highlights the longstanding commitment to education held by many Black Christians. The author uses this case study and two others to unpack the manner in which the relationship between churches and institutions of higher learning informed and influenced the full range of life experiences for African Americans in the deep south resulting in the growth of a Black professional class.

Keywords: Trans-Atlantic slave trade; emancipation proclamation; protest; Baptist Student Union; Mt. Gilead Baptist Church; Houston

'Saving' Education, pages 7–28
Copyright © 2025 by Emerald Publishing Limited
All rights of reproduction in any form reserved.
doi:10.1108/978-1-83708-894-220251002

Discussions about African American history often begin with a focus on the Trans-Atlantic Slave Trade and the resulting dispersals of people of African descent throughout the Americas, including "Tejas, Mexico," now Texas, United States of America. Notwithstanding the historical significance of an exchange that endured for approximately 400 years, research affirms that emancipated Blacks in Texas took measurable steps to lift themselves out of poverty by creating and nurturing a dynamic educational and professional exchange comprised of interconnected individuals and organizations committed to progress. The educational, professional, and political exchanges examined in this essay emerged out of the "Black Church," which W. E. B. DuBois famously referred to as "the birthplace of the Negro Masses."

Black churches in Texas, often established by formerly enslaved men and women, became launchpads for non-profit and for-profit institutions, including schools, universities, burial societies, insurance agencies, newspapers, hat shops, restaurants, and beauty and barber schools. Most of these churches had humble beginnings shaped by determined members who pooled their resources together in creative ways. The degree to which their undertakings were successful depended on church leaders' educational attainment, members' individual and collective commitment to educational outreach and social advancement, organizational culture, and the geopolitical environments in which they operated.[1]

Texas was a fertile field for imagining, encouraging, and creating opportunities for vibrant social and political exchange. The Emancipation Proclamation and General Order 3, the acclaimed Juneteenth document, effectuated the release of approximately 250,000 Blacks in Texas. In the early years of the 20th century, Black migrants also poured into Texas from Louisiana, Mississippi, Alabama, and other former slave states. By 1906, people of African descent formed majorities in 14 counties along the Texas coast, in the Brazos River valley, and in Northeast Texas, and constituted 40–50% of the population in 13 other East Texas counties.[2] According to "Progress of the Negro in Texas," a report prepared for the Bureau of the Census by Charles E. Hall, the Black religious community was diverse and dynamic. Hall noted the following:

> ...in 1926 there were 3,910 black churches in Texas with a total membership of 351,305. Of the 3,539 church edifices, 3,506 reported a total value of $10, 587, 143 or an average of $3,020 per church. The 3,376 churches reporting Sunday schools contained 26, 297 officers and teachers and 167,193 scholars. The Baptist bodies led in the number of members, followed by the African American Episcopal Church, the Methodist Episcopal Church, the Colored Methodist Episcopal Church, the Roman Catholic Church, and the Church of God in Christ.[3]

Many of the "teachers" and "scholars" referenced in Hall's report were educated in a variety of private and public institutions established to educate Blacks in Texas. From 1872 to 1950, approximately 11 historically Black colleges and universities (HBCUs) were established in Texas with each playing a key role in the educational and professional development of Blacks in the Lone Star State. Methodist polities established the earliest institutions of higher learning for Blacks in Texas, with the African Methodist Episcopal Church leading the way by establishing Paul Quinn College in Dallas, TX, in 1872. Please see the table below:

Paul Quinn College	Dallas	1872	African Methodist Episcopal
Wiley College	Marshall	1873	Methodist Episcopal
Huston-Tillotson University	Austin	1875	United Methodist Church
Prairie View A & M University	Prairie View	1876	The First State Public School
Bishop College	Marshall	1881	Baptist
Texas College	Tyler	1894	Christian Methodist Episcopal
St. Philips College	San Antonio	1898	Protestant Episcopal Church
Jarvis Christian College	Hawkins	1913	Christian Church (Disciples of Christ)
Thurgood Marshall School of Law	Houston	1946	Public Law School
Texas Southern University	Houston	1947	Public School
Southwestern Christian College	Georgetown	1948	Churches of Christ

Based on a variety of sources and digital archives, this essay examines the distinct ways in which selected leaders and members of three Black Baptist churches, among the thousands established in Texas, created or collaborated with educational institutions and organizations to promote the social, economic, and political advancement of Blacks in Texas from the late 19th century onwards. In *Politics in the Pews*, Eric McDaniel posits that "a politicized church represents the end result of the negotiation process between the leadership and members."[4] This negotiation process is also impacted by organizational culture and the environment within and beyond the walls of the church. McDaniel's framework is useful in this study, which examines the community engagement models of three prominent Black churches whose dates of establishment span a 117-year period: Mt. Gilead Baptist Church, established in Fort Worth, TX, in 1875; Pleasant Hill Baptist Church, established in Houston, TX, in 1925; and Wheeler Avenue Baptist Church, established in Houston, TX, in 1962. The leadership and members of each congregation responded to the sociopolitical developments of their time. Mt. Gilead Baptist Church was established during Reconstruction, Pleasant Hill Baptist Church, during the Great Migration, and Wheeler

Avenue Baptist Church, during the Great Migration and civil rights movement. Each church rose to prominence and figured among the 115 or more Baptist churches in Texas that were directly or loosely affiliated with the National Baptist Convention, USA, Inc., where early leaders emphasized "productivity" over "protest."[5] This general position was consistently maintained until a rising tide of youth, educated in separate-but-unequal schools, pushed their conservative elders to help them fight for social and political change. From Reconstruction through most of the Great Migration, the mission was clear: educate, produce, and become economically self-sufficient. When the doors of economic opportunity remained stubbornly closed, workers and students demanded change.

THE EDUCATIONAL AND PROFESSIONAL EXCHANGE: THE CASE OF MT. GILEAD BAPTIST CHURCH (1875), PRAIRIE VIEW A & M (1876), I. M. TERRELL HIGH SCHOOL (1882), THE COLORED TEACHERS STATE ASSOCIATION OF TEXAS (1884)

Archival material from Prairie View A & M's Digital Commons reveals a vibrant educational and professional exchange between Mt. Gilead Baptist Church (1875), Prairie View A & M (1876), I. M. Terrell High School (1882), and the Colored Teachers State Association of Texas, which was active from 1884 to 1948. One man stood at the nexus of the exchange: Isaiah Milligen Terrell (1859–1931), a dedicated member of Mt. Gilead Baptist Church. Mt. Gilead Baptist Church was established by formerly enslaved Blacks like Terrell and became a vibrant force for educational and professional exchange. The church boasted several thousand members in its heyday and impacted the lives of African Americans throughout the State of Texas and beyond. Early pastors, including Lacey Kirk Williams, and early church members valued education and collaboration, and they emphasized the importance of self-reliance and economic progress.

Thanks to Terrell's effort and that of other founding members, Mt. Gilead establish a private church school that formed the nucleus for East Ninth Street Colored School, the first public school for Blacks in Fort Worth and the only one for Blacks in Tarrant County. Terrell, a graduate of Prairie View A & M, served as Superintendent of Mt. Gilead's Sunday School and the church school's first principal. In honor of I. M. Terrell's dynamic leadership, East Ninth Street Colored School was eventually renamed "I. M. Terrell School" in 1921.[6] The staff and student body grew under Terrell's leadership, and included a host of stellar students like Lillian Ackard Jones Horace (1880–1965), a pioneering teacher, librarian, and Texas's earliest known African American female novelist and Lulu B. White (1907–1957), teacher and civil rights activist. The impact of their efforts would be evident in the activism of one of Terrell's most recently celebrated graduates, Opal Lee (1926–), a.k.a., "The Grandmother of Juneteenth."

I. M. Terrell leveraged his institutional affiliations to help foster opportunities for dynamic exchanges between the church and educational institutions. No doubt because of his influence, Mt. Gilead Baptist Church, became a hub for educational and professional empowerment. Mt. Gilead hosted the 48th annual meeting of the "Colored Teachers' State Association of Texas" on November 24–26, 1932. Established in 1884, the organization had members in approximately 26 cities throughout Texas by 1939 and 40 cities by 1952. I. M. Terrell high school students were exposed to the proceedings, as a mixed chorus from I. M. Terrell High School performed at the gathering.[7] Lillian Jones Horace served as second vice president of the Colored Teachers' State Association of Texas. Horace's younger colleague, Hazel Harvey Peace, after whom a reading room at the Fort Worth Public Library is named, served in the same capacity until the organization closed with the emergence of integration.

The collective impact of organizations like the Association and the Black southern churches that supported them was significant. The enrollment of Black students at normal schools and colleges throughout the South increased 500% between 1916 and 1927. According to *The Crisis*, there were 19,000 Blacks enrolled in colleges and universities throughout the United States in 1930. Of this number, 1,707 earned bachelor's degrees, 289 earned professional degrees, and 76, the master's or PhD. The impact was evident in Texas. According to the 1930 Census, Black educators in Texas were making important strides. Blacks constituted 14% of the population in the Lone Star State and attained a literacy rate of 86.6%, the highest of any Southern state.[8] Equally important, in 1932, 2,973 Black students were enrolled in teacher training programs at public and private institutions.[9]

Because of the ready connections between Terrell, Horace, and Mt. Gilead, I. M. Terrell High School served as a pipeline and collaborative partner for students and faculty at Prairie View A & M University. This was a remarkable achievement, as Prairie View, the first state-supported institution of higher learning for African Americans, was established after the Civil War during Reconstruction on land that had once served as a slave plantation.[10] From 1936 to 1958, four Prairie View undergraduate research projects resulted from collaborations with administrators, faculty, staff, or students affiliated with I. M. Terrell. The research projects respectively treated social studies (1936), history pedagogy (1940), family life education (1953), and intramural sports (1958). In 1951, of the 12 institutions represented among staff at I. M. Terrell, Prairie View tied with Wiley College for the most alumni working there.[11] I. M. Terrell's standard of excellence was long established thanks to the early foundation work of the school's first principal and namesake. Terrell's outstanding leadership at East Ninth Colored High made him the perfect candidate to become the fifth principal of Prairie View A & M, which thrived under his leadership from 1915 to 1918.[12]

By 1917, the year before Terrell's tenure ended, Prairie View housed the "second largest physical plant of any Negro school in the country, the largest college auditorium of any Negro school in the state, 46 teachers and officers on its regular staff, and an enrollment of 978 students."[13] By 1918, when Terrell's tenure at Prairie View ended, Prairie View had become a senior college. Terrell continued to exercise his commitment to administration and institution-building. In 1918, Terrell moved to Houston, TX, where he served as president of Houston College (Houston Baptist Academy) for approximately five years. In 1923, Terrell was named superintendent of the Union Hospital. In 1925, he retired from Houston College and worked to secure funds to established Houston Negro Hospital, later named Riverside General Hospital. He was named the first superintendent of the hospital at its dedication in 1926. He also became superintendent emeritus of the same institution in 1928. Terrell died on September 28, 1931, in Houston, Texas. He was laid to rest in College Park Cemetery, a historic Black cemetery located in Houston's historic Fourth Ward. The productive model for educational and professional exchange that Terrell forged between Mt. Gilead Baptist Church, Prairie View A & M, I. M. Terrell High School, and the Colored Teachers Association of Texas flourished throughout the Jim Crow Era and laid the educational and professional foundation for a robust generation of Black educators, business owners, and community leaders. As one writer noted, "As a builder of concerns with which he was connected, [Isaiah Milligen Terrell] had but few equals."[14]

THE PROFESSIONAL, FRATERNAL, AND POLITICAL EXCHANGE: LEE HAYWOOD SIMPSON AND PLEASANT HILL BAPTIST CHURCH, HOUSTON (FIFTH WARD), TX (1925–1967)

While the educational and professional exchange involving Mt. Gilead Baptist Church, I. M. Terrell High School, Prairie View A & M, and the Colored Teachers Association of Texas pivoted on the leadership of I. M. Terrell, a pioneering member of Mt. Gilead Baptist Church, the productive exchanges that emerged at Pleasant Hill Baptist Church, Houston, TX, stemmed from the business, fraternal, and professional connections of Lee Haywood Simpson, the founding pastor of Pleasant Hill Baptist Church. Simpson used his connections with fraternal and professional organizations, businessmen, and civil rights leaders to make Pleasant Hill Baptist Church one of the most progressive Black congregations in Houston during the Jim Crow era.[15] Simpson was not extensively educated when he started pastoring, but he understood the importance of education, encouraged youth to obtain an education, helped Pleasant Hill establish an educational building, and helped fund the education of at least one graduate of Texas Southern University (TSU). Accordingly, the relationship between Pleasant Hill Baptist Church and Texas Southern University was not forged formally at an administrative level as in the case of Mt. Gilead Baptist Church and Prairie View A & M or Wheeler Avenue Baptist Church and Texas Southern University. Ties between Pleasant Hill and Texas Southern were established informally through church members who happened to attend or work at Texas Southern.

Lee Haywood Simpson was born July 20, 1884, in Calvert, TX. His family moved from Robertson County for better opportunity and to escape increased violence against Blacks in many rural communities in Texas. He graduated from Conroe Industrial and Normal School[16] in the early 1900s and completed doctoral studies later in life.[17] Houston did not have a comprehensive set of rules or "Black codes" when his family arrived. The behavior and social interactions of Blacks were controlled by an uneven series of state laws and local ordinances designed to keep the races apart. Yet, the city took steps to control and disenfranchise its growing Black population. Travel restrictions were imposed in 1903 and 1907. By 1910, the office of the Houston Democratic Party had established its presence on Lyons Avenue down the street from Pleasant Hill Baptist Church. By 1921, the Houston Democratic Party had passed a law stipulating that only white men could vote in the Democratic Primary. Later, in 1922, the city instituted regulations to keep Blacks and whites in separate parks. In 1923, the state of Texas followed suit. The year before the state mandated segregated recreational facilities, in 1922, Jack Yates and other ministers established Emancipation Park in Houston's Third Ward, the first park established for African Americans in the city, four miles south of Pleasant Hill. By 1940, both the Lyons and Deluxe Theaters had been constructed for Black audiences in response to segregation laws.

Houston grew rapidly after the Civil War, as many African American southerners left small-town life and peonage systems of labor to find better educational and professional opportunities.[18] The discovery of oil in Beaumont in 1900 precipitated growth. The population increased from 44,633 in 1900 to approximately 138,276 in 1920, which led to growth in infrastructure, including hotels, office buildings, apartment houses, streetcars, waterworks, telephones, telegraphs, theaters, a public library, and social organizations. Economic progress notwithstanding, when Simpson and other Black southerners migrated to Houston, they entered a segregated city where Blacks were marginalized. They could not vote and found very few opportunities to improve their circumstances. Black Houstonians were taught to be submissive and deferential on the job, as well as in their contact with whites in public. Despite Houston's segregationist practices, Blacks found more economic opportunity in Houston than in the rural areas from which they migrated, whether they journeyed from East Texas towns or Louisiana. Many migrated to the Fifth Ward region, where the Black population increased from 578 to 4,967 from 1870 to 1910, making it one of the fastest-growing Black residential wards in Houston.

Simpson's mother worked as a laundry woman to support he and his sister, Alice. Three other siblings preceded him in death. Although Simpson's mother could not read or write, she valued education and made sure Simpson attended church and school. Accordingly, he grew up in Pleasant Grove Baptist Church, a prominent church in Fifth Ward. When Simpson's mother's economic situation grew worse, he curtailed his own education to help support his mother and other family members. On November 30, 1910, Simpson married Lela H. Elder, who was born in Hempstead, TX, in 1895, and was 15 years younger than Simpson. The couple resided in Fifth Ward at 1513 Gregg Street and bore two children, Lee and Lela. Simpson, a hard-working young man, secured a job as a porter at Mosehart & Kellery, a buggy repair and horseshoeing operation in 1891 and later secured a job at a car dealership.

After his tenure at Mosehart & Kellery, Simpson worked for Pierce-Arrow Motor Car Company at 1710 Main St., where many of his customers were affluent, influential whites. Although Jim Crow customs limited his engagement, he developed and maintained relationships with many prominent whites. Simpson began working at Pierce-Arrow in 1917, the same year the Houston Riot occurred. On Saturday, July 17, 1917, white men assaulted a Black woman. Asserting that the police officers had not responded appropriately, approximately 100 Black soldiers affiliated with the Third Battalion of the 24th Infantry in Houston, marched on the city, killed 16 whites and wounded approximately 12. As a result, 13 Black soldiers were executed at Fort Sam Houston, on December 11, 1917, and 40 were sentenced to life in prison. The riot occurred August 23, 1917, the same year Lee H. Simpson signed his United States World War I draft registration card (September 18, 1918). However, there is no evidence Simpson actually served in the military. This limited contact provided Simpson with a unique perspective on race relations in Houston.

Booker T. Washington visited Houston and spoke in the City Auditorium to 7,000 affluent Blacks and whites. Charles Norvell Love, editor of the *Texas Freeman*, was in charge of arrangements. There is no evidence that Simpson attended, but it is reasonable to speculate that he was aware of its occurrence because of his interactions with people in high places in his church and in the community. Lela Simpson had lived in 4th Ward, where the first library accessible to Blacks was established in 1907. Houston's own Emmett J. Scott, the first editor of the *Texas Freeman*, worked as an aide to Booker T. Washington. It was Scott's connection with Washington from which emerged the Andrew Carnegie connection. In 1910, Andrew Carnegie appropriated 15,000 dollars to build a "Colored Library."

By 1920, Simpson had started a small business and developed a keen business sense. His business allowed him to connect with Blacks and influential whites like Oscar Holcombe. Simpson entered the lumber business perhaps because of his relationship with Holcombe, who became very wealthy and understood the importance of real estate ownership and political connections. Holcombe ran for Mayor, won, and served 11 terms, but not consecutively. In December 1921, 2000 white men were inducted into the Ku Klux Klan in Bellaire. Holcombe joined but resigned after attending one meeting. Simpson did not sever ties with him.

Simpson attended Pleasant Grove Baptist Church, where he served as a trustee for 22 years. He also served as Secretary and Superintendent of the Sunday School, where he encouraged children to get an education and developed a zeal for Christian education. Because of his service, he was ordained as a deacon. While completing work on a jobsite in Port Arthur, Texas, Simpson received what he referred to as a "call from the Lord." Although there were no strict educational requirements to pastor, the general custom was to study under the current Pastor and then become licensed and ordained. In 1925, Simpson pastored Watts Chapel Baptist Church. Watts's six members congregated in a building that was 18 × 22 feet. Once established, the members decided to rename the church "Pleasant Hill Baptist Church." The congregation then announced Simpson as its leader. His service as pastor proved to be foundational for his role as an advocate and activist for civil rights, as well as for building his base as a leader.

A professional, Simpson used a business model to conduct church affairs. He was an eloquent speaker and delivered charismatic sermons. He also knew the economic and social needs of Fifth Ward residents and used that knowledge strategically when members joined. He kept a detailed census of members, including biographical details and place of employment. He used the data collected to help build a new edifice. By 1933, during the Great Depression, Pleasant Hill had 1,183 members and the mortgage for the first church expansion was paid off in its entirety by December 31 of the same year. The total cost was $8,716, which included $1,850 in interest. The establishment of Pleasant Hill was only the beginning of Simpson's influence. In 1940, Pleasant Hill added an educational building, increasing the property value to $50,000. Simpson's relationships helped him raise funds to complete the work from Parking Building & Lumbar, Alamo Steel, and the Colored Ministers Association.

Simpson gained the trust of various leaders and organizations, including members of the National Association for the Advancement of Colored People (NAACP), Negro Chamber of Commerce, Gibraltar Mutual Life Insurance, and the General Baptist Congress. Ministers respected law and order but wanted justice for Blacks. Simpson became president of the association in 1929. Members of the association held that

...every citizen has the inherent and constitutional right to resist with every honorable and lawful means any pressure by means of force or design which tends to force about their minds, hands, or feet....in any form...the shackles of enslavement, or badge of inferiority.

The Houston branch of the NAACP was established in 1913, but it became active after the riot of 1917. The Negro Chamber of Commerce was formed to support Black businesses and the Texas Interracial Committee aimed to work with liberal thinking whites. Black groups, including the Progressive Voter's League and the Independent Voter's League, were established in response to a faction of the Republican Party, the Lily-White Republicans, which desired to remove Blacks from its ranks. Lulu B. White encourage Simpson to run for public office. Lulu White was a graduate of I. M. Terrell High School, Fort Worth, TX, and Prairie View A & M, and she was a member of Antioch Baptist Church, founded in Houston's Freedman's Town by the legendary Reverend Jack Yates.[19]

In 1946, Simpson ran for City Council. Rather than represent 5th Ward, he ran for an "at-large" position as an independent, making him the first Black to do so in Houston. Simpson had the backing of labor unions but lost the election. He nonetheless became president of the Houston branch of the NAACP. He supported Lulu B. White and her effort to integrate the University of Texas Law School via *Sweatt v. Painter* (1950). He eventually encountered problems in the NAACP and lost his position as president, but he continued to work on behalf of Pleasant Hill Baptist Church. For his service, in 1947, he was given life tenure as pastor.

Simpson took a non-confrontational approach to equality. He believed in civil rights but thought economic progress was most important. His position was consistent with that of many Black southerners, including Booker T. Washington, and early members of the National Baptist Convention, USA, Inc. He believed Blacks should work hard and respect their white neighbors. He also believed in self-help and urged Blacks to establish their own businesses and become financially independent from the white community. He understood that Black churches were responsible for a variety of economic enterprises. He also knew they had limited economic opportunity, so he used his knowledge to help Blacks become entrepreneurs. He permitted businessmen to advertise in church bulletins, including Judson Robinson and Mack Hannah. Judson Robinson, a prominent and vocal resident of Fifth Ward, was the son of a Baptist minister and was born in 1907 in Crockett, TX. Robinson founded Judson W. Robinson & Sons Real Estate Mortgage Company, the first Black mortgage company in the state to be approved by the Federal Housing Authority. Robinson was also a member of Pleasant Hill Men's Business League.

Simpson also established a business relationship with Mack Hannah, of Port Arthur, TX, who studied at Bishop College, an HBCU affiliated with the National Baptist Convention, USA, Inc. Hannah, a casket salesman, founded Mack Hannah Life Insurance and served on the Board of Directors at Texas Southern University.[20] Simpson and Hannah were active in the NAACP and the Young Men's Christian Association, and they belonged to the fraternal order of the Masons. Hannah supported Simpson's effort to build "New Waverly Christian Home for the Aged and Orphans" at New Waverly, Texas, Walker County. Business leaders sought Hannah's support. So, too, did organizations like the General Baptist State Congress, and the National Baptist Convention of America.

In keeping with his non-confrontational approach to civil rights, Simpson was "a vocal opponent of the sit-ins." He did not support civil disobedience or angry displays of public agitation, but he criticized injustice and challenged members of the Minister's Association to welcome the changing times. He noted,

> This new age has produced a new Negro who, no longer will sit supinely by and allow the American white man's assumed superiority and supremacy to go unchallenged. The new Negro is not going to give up his fight for equality. All forms of racialism, prejudice, and injustice are undesirable and unacceptable to the Negroes of the USA.[21]

In response to President John F. Kennedy's assassination on November 23, 1963, Simpson helped arrange a public demonstration for freedom and racial equality. Approximately 500–600 African Americans and 50 whites marched in support of the civil rights movement. Simpson noted, "Anybody that can beat you thinking can enslave you. We never will be able to do anything in Houston until we Negroes organize."[22] Simpson died of carbon-monoxide poisoning November 8, 1967. He was 83 years old. More than 1,000 people attended the funeral of the "Clever Preacher" who used his business acumen and professional networks to promote social change.

THE EDUCATIONAL AND POLITICAL EXCHANGE: WHEELER AVENUE BAPTIST CHURCH AND TEXAS SOUTHERN UNIVERSITY, 1955 TO THE PRESENT

The final exchange to be examined in this essay involves Wheeler Avenue Baptist Church and Texas Southern University, and it emerged during a pivotal time in American history. Even though Wheeler Avenue Baptist Church was not an active member of the National Baptist Convention, USA, Wheeler Avenue's founding pastor and wife team, William "Bill" Lawson and Audrey Lawson, and other Black Baptists in Houston were aware of the convention's position on issues facing African Americans in the 1960s.

The most pressing concerns were on the agenda of the 82nd annual meeting of the National Baptist Convention, USA, Inc., which met in Chicago, Illinois, in 1962, the same year Wheeler Avenue Baptist Church was founded.

President Joseph H. Jackson outlined his concerns for "world peace," "America," "our own racial struggle," "the sin of degradation," and the importance of "facing the future with God."[23] In response to the civil rights movement, Jackson admonished his audience to pursue economic opportunity—to "produce" rather than "protest" because protest could not change minds or hearts. Approximately 115 Texas Black Baptist churches were present to consider Jackson's conservative approach, including Mt. Gilead Baptist Church, several other Fort Worth churches and associations, and at least five churches from Houston—Antioch Baptist Church (Reverend E. R. Boone, 318 Andrews St.); Bethel (Reverend W. H. Dudley, 2,607 Chartres St.), Lincoln Southern District Association (Rev. W. H. Dudley, 2,607 Chartres St.), Grace Temple (Rev. E. E. Potts, 842 West 22nd St), and New Hope (Rev. M. M. Pierson, 1221 Crockett).

The response to Jackson's address was mixed. Some heard and received Jackson's message; others heard it but were not prepared to heed it. Other NBC Convention members were proud that their organization had more civil rights leaders than "any other denomination in America." The growing list included Ralph Abernathy, Wm. Borders, Jerry Dayton, Nathaniel Ellis, E. S. Evans, J. H. Jackson, B. Joseph Johnson, Mordecai W. Johnson, Martin Luther King, Benjamin E. Mays, Jr., J. M. Nabrit, Gardner Taylor, A. Clayton Powell, Fred Shuttlesworth, Kelley Miller Smith, C. K. Steele, L. M. Terrill, C. A. T. Walden, Wyatt T. Walker, Sr., and Roger Williams.[24] Joseph M. Nabrit, President of Howard University, spoke at one of the sessions. President Joseph M. Nabrit was also the brother of Samuel M. Nabrit, the second president of Texas Southern University.

The differences were perceived to be so great that some, like Martin Luther King, eventually parted ways with the National Baptist Convention and joined L. Venchael Booth, who had established the Progressive National Baptist Convention in 1961. Booth's inspiration was rooted in Williams's definitive biography, *Crowned With Glory and Honor: The Life of Reverend Lacy Kirk Williams*, which Lillian Jones Horace, Mt. Gilead Baptist Church, had written 20 years earlier and prayed "the Baptist" would publish. Booth edited, published, and presented Horace's work at the 1964 annual meeting of the Progressive Baptist Convention, one year before Horace died. He published Horace's work a second time in 1974.

Baptist influence was welcomed at Texas Southern University, where President Samuel Nabrit served as president from 1955 to 1966. Nabrit was the first Morehouse graduate to earn a doctoral degree, the first Black to earn a PhD from Brown University, and the first Black to serve as a trustee at the same institution.[25] Suggesting his influence, Dr. Nabrit was appointed by President John F. Kennedy as a special delegate to represent the United States at the Nigerian Independence celebration, December 16–18, 1961.[26] As he was an alumnus of Morehouse College, one of the private colleges supported by the National Baptist Convention, it may have been natural for him to promote Christian education and chaplaincy at Texas Southern despite Texas Southern University's designation as a public school. Nabrit's administration demonstrated a commitment to the spiritual growth and development of TSU students by supporting "Religious Emphasis Week," in which religious leaders on campus, professors, students, and guests participated. His approach was common among private HBCUs, 55% of which were established and funded by religious denominations.

The influence of various religious polities on private and public HBCU campuses ranged from integral to tangential.[27] When William "Bill" Alexander Lawson initiated his period of service as Director of the Baptist Student Union at Texas Southern University, the Supreme Court had ruled against state-endorsed prayer in public schools in *Engel v. Vitale (1962)*, but it did not ban the establishment of student-led religious organizations on college campuses. Among the various religious organizations active on the TSU campus in the 1960s were the Lutheran Student Association, Young Men's Christian Association, Wesley Foundation, Student Association for Church of Christ,[28] Young Women's Christian Association,[29] and the COGIC Club (Church of God in Christ). Advisors and chaplains contributed to student life by participating in programs held throughout the year. For example, Reverend Julius Scott, Methodist student director, delivered the Thanksgiving message in 1962.[30]

The individual and collective efforts of TSU chaplains and advisors also extended beyond the Texas Southern University campus. Dr. A. J. Hines of Houston, who served as advisor of the COGIC Club, went on to play a leading role in establishing the system of Bible colleges for the Church of God in Christ. Dr. Hines organized a pilot school in Houston that became a model for the nearly 40 schools established throughout the United States.[31] Students also received words of inspiration from guest ministers, including Reverend John Patrick Murray, of the Augustana Lutheran Church, who participated in the 14th annual commencement exercises,[32] and Dr. William H. King, professor of Preaching, McCormick Theological Seminary, Chicago, who delivered the keynote address.

Of the religious organizations noted, the Baptist Student Union stood out for its emphasis on the role that "adults" played in an organization with ecumenical sensibilities. The following description was posted in the 1962 yearbook:

> The Baptist Student Union is not so much an organization of Baptist students as a movement among concerned adult Baptists to minister to the spiritual needs of all students. This ministry performs through weekly seminar discussions, fellowship luncheons, daily prayer experiences and periodic

intercampus contacts, with students throughout the state and nation and various other activities and emphasis seeks to yield at the end of the college generation, a more finished human being prepared to serve with Christian dignity and loyalty to the church of Jesus Christ.[33]

William Lawson filled the bill. He may have helped author the description, as he served as chaplain at the date of its publishing. Notwithstanding the Baptist Student Union's stated emphasis on the students' spiritual lives, the students' concern for civil rights helped Lawson refine and adopt a Christian theology that pivoted not only on a vertical relationship with heaven, but also on a horizontal relationship with the community.

Lawson was born June 28, 1928, in St. Louis, Missouri, and he attended Frederick Douglass Elementary in Webster Groves, Missouri. With encouragement from some of his teachers, he became a good student in Northeast Junior High School and an excellent student in high school at Summer Academy of Arts and Sciences, both in Kansas City, Kansas. After graduating from high school, he attended Tennessee Agricultural and Industrial State College, now Tennessee State University, in Nashville, where his academic performance was "more average."[34] After completing his studies at Tennessee State, he attended Central Baptist Theological Seminary in Kansas City, Kansas.[35] Lawson was exposed to a variety of religious expressions in his youth, which prepared him to help manage the fault lines—even landmines—between the various religious polities and communities in Fifth Ward, where he worshiped before founding Wheeler Avenue Baptist Church in Houston's Third Ward, and at Texas Southern, where he served as chaplain, as well as in the Greater Houston community. Lawson came to embrace the Baptist faith because his stepfather, Walter Cade, was a very active member of the National Baptist Convention, USA, Inc. In his youth, Lawson was active in the choir, served as a part-time church janitor, and participated in church youth movements.

Lawson's wife, Audrey Lawson, was born on March 20, 1932, in St. Louis, Missouri, to John Henry and Alma Hoffman. She attended elementary and secondary schools in St. Louis. She began her college education at Stowe Teacher's College and transferred to Tennessee State University in Nashville, Tennessee, and graduated with a BA in social work after William Lawson had left Tennessee State. She and William Lawson met through correspondence while she was still at Tennessee State. Their now historic courtship is captured in 600 letters housed at the African American Library at the Gregory School in Houston, TX.[36]

The couple's unique educational and experiential preparation readied them for the long life of service that their time at Texas Southern University engendered. Similar to Mt. Gilead Baptist Church of Fort Worth, TX, which was founded in the wake of the Emancipation, Wheeler was established during the early stages of desegregation and integration. When the Lawsons arrived, the Third Ward Community was in flux. Reflecting patterns of white flight that occurred throughout the city of Houston, Jewish residence had begun to move out as African Americans moved in. Wheeler Avenue's founding members were all African American newcomers to the region. Some were employed by Texas Southern University and the Houston Independent School District. As there were no Black Baptist churches near campus, Lawson tried to find a church that would establish a satellite for TSU students and for the young families that were gradually moving into the newly integrated area. When no established congregation agreed to plant a satellite, Bill and Audrey Lawson started holding a one-hour, student-centered gathering in their home. The short service began at 10.00 a.m. and ended at 11.00 a.m. to accommodate the students' study schedules and allow founding members, including the Lawsons, to meet their respective obligations at their home churches in Fifth Ward.

From 1955 to 1961, Lawson and the students he and his wife advised had to grapple with some of the most iconic developments of the modern civil rights movement. Bill and Audrey Lawson joined TSU on August 28, 1955, the same day Emmett Till was murdered in Mississippi. Till's murder strengthened Rosa Park's resolve to participate in the Montgomery Boycotts, which began on December 5, 1955, 100 days after Till's murder.[37] Till's demise also inspired students throughout the country to get involved. TSU students were determined to join the struggle. Inspired by sit-ins staged by students from North Carolina A & T, on February 1, 1960, TSU students asked Lawson to help them desegregate the lunch counter of a local grocery store.[38] Lawson was hesitant. He explained, "I was National Baptist but was pretty well Southern Baptist and we simply did not get involved in stuff like that." The Southern Baptist Convention Lawson referenced was a predominantly white organization. Lawson was among the local Black pastors who began to join the Southern Baptist Convention after the demise of de jure segregation.[39]

Given his conservative leanings, Lawson tried to dissuade the students by reminding them of their original purpose to earn a college degree. However, the students stated succinctly that if Lawson would not help them, they would find someone else. He recalled,

> They walked out of the Baptist Student Center and left me standing there. In the next hour, they were down at a local supermarket that had some lunch counters. They sat...at these lunch counters and they were thrown in jail.

He further recalled:

> ... Audrey and I were introduced to the Civil Rights Movement, first of all by our–by our bewilderment by the determination of these students, and secondly by the fact that somebody had to get them out of jail. And she and a couple of neighbors on that street and I went out raising money to bail these kids out. That was how we began our involvement in civil rights. After that we did become involved in civil rights, but it started then.

TSU students organized the first "sit-in" to desegregate lunch counters in Houston, on March 4, 1960. On August 25, 1960, Houston lunch counters "quietly desegregated."[40] The Lawsons' support endeared them to the students. By 1961, the group that met at their home had gelled into a "church family." Because Lawson was a chaplain and had limited experience with pastoring, he agreed to serve only as the interim pastor until the group found a pastor. Lawson recalled that neighborhood residents approached him saying:

> You're...a student chaplain and so you're a preacher. Will you help us establish a church? And once again, as...was the case with the students who wanted me to give them direction for civil rights, my feeling was that...I was there to be a student chaplain, that I was not a pastor, except for this tiny church in Pittsburg [Kansas] I'd never been a pastor. And so...I'd be glad to help them find somebody who would be pastor of a church.

Lawson made good on his promise and found Prentice Moore, "a very brilliant young fella" who was then named pastor of what congregants called "Riverside [Riverside Baptist Church]." The group stopped meeting in the Lawsons' home and relocated to a "little white [vacant] building" on 3826 Wheeler Avenue. The seller of the edifice was a member of the Southern Baptist Convention and appreciated the congregation's effort to establish a place of worship for students at nearby Texas Southern. He sold the edifice to the congregation interest-free and at an extremely low price. Thus, Wheeler Avenue Baptist Church was established and ready to expand its work in the Third Ward community. Lawson was to serve as Prentice Moore's advisor. However, after six months of service, Moore received a call from a seminary indicating he had been awarded a scholarship to return to seminary. Moore asked Lawson what he should do, and Lawson advised him to go to seminary and assured him that he would hold the church until Moore returned. Lawson added, "He never got back, so I remained as pastor of Wheeler Avenue Baptist Church for some forty-two years."

As its unique congregational formation suggests, Wheeler's emergence was different from that of traditional Baptist churches, which are congregationally governed. Baptist Pastors (then always male) were generally hired to direct the church. The congregation could also fire the pastor. The Lawsons' direct engagement in the early phases of the church's development resembled the formation pattern exhibited by a growing number of independent churches, which were established by husband-and-wife teams in historic Black communities as well as in the newly integrated ones that emerged throughout the city of Houston from the 1950s onwards. Lawson described Wheeler's theology as one established on a vertical relationship between the individual and heaven, and a horizontal relationship between the individual and his fellow man. He noted,

So while [Wheeler] did have to have a strong bond with God, it also had to reach out to work with people who were poor, who were segregated, who were undereducated, and so for that reason, Wheeler has always had a strong social outreach, and my background in sociology didn't hurt.

Audrey Ann Hoffman Lawson's (1932–2015) background was also a benefit as she helped Wheeler establish the William A. Lawson Institute for Peace and Prosperity (WALIPP Institute), which eventually established a school for inner city boys and a retirement facility.

Wheeler Avenue's geographical location is equally significant to the church's history and mission. Tierwester, the other thoroughfare, and Wheeler Avenue, were closed at the points where the streets cross the TSU campus to create the "Tigerwalk extension," which was completed in 2012.[41] The Wheeler Avenue Baptist Church's now 80,000-foot complex stands on the corner of Scott St. and Wheeler, east of the Tigerwalk and within walking distance of Texas Southern, the University of Houston, and iconic symbols of African American history located on or near Scott St., including Frenchy's, the first Black-owned Burger King franchise in Houston, Jack Yates High School, the Lonnie Smith Library, and other emblems of Black history in third Ward.

Wheeler Avenue extended its reach to the community from a place of higher learning—a university—and with an ever-expanding commitment to improve the lives of Blacks in the Third Ward community.[42] The Lawsons' support for the sit-ins was an important beginning for the church's ongoing commitment to community uplift. Although Lawson never marched with Dr. Martin Luther King, he hosted King at Wheeler Avenue Baptist Church when other local pastors refused to do so. Lawson also founded an Southern Christian Leadership Conference local office at Dr. King's request. As Lawson was considered to be a voice of reason, local leaders reached out to him in turbulent times, and there were many in quick succession locally, regionally, and nationally. John F. Kennedy was assassinated in nearby Dallas, on November 22, 1963, the day after Kennedy had waved to students at Fort Worth's historic I. M. Terrell High School. The Civil Rights Act of 1964 was passed by the Johnson Administration, but racial tensions were far from resolved. In response to its passage, Lawson led a march against school segregation in Houston. On February 21, 1965, Malcolm X was murdered. On May 16, 1967, a riot erupted on the TSU campus. Lawson attempted to assuage students' concerns but to no avail. The students fired shots at the police and the police unloaded 1,000 rounds into the dormitory wall. Local newspapers did not cover the riot but published a story about the students' convictions. On April 4, 1968, Dr. Martin Luther King was assassinated at the Lorraine Motel, in Memphis, TN. His death stunned the nation but did not silence the call for justice. Political change was afoot. The Voting Rights Act of 1965 opened the door for professional Black politicians to take their positions in what had become a long marathon for justice.

An unprecedented number of elected officials emerged in Texas, including legendary TSU graduates such as Congresswoman Barbara Jordan, Congressman Mickey Leland, State Representative Al Edwards, the father of Juneteenth, and a host of others who pursued careers in public service.

The Lawsons' student-inspired focus on civil rights was an education in and of itself. It impacted and engaged a host of future teachers, administrators, and community leaders, some of whom have served with distinction on the TSU campus. Wheeler member Robert J. Terry served as interim president of Texas Southern University in 1986. During his tenure as president, The College of Pharmacy awarded Texas Southern University's first Doctor of Pharmacy degree.[43] Dr. Patricia Williams, current Director of Spiritual Life at Wheeler Avenue Baptist Church, served as a professor of English at Texas Southern University. Over the course of her extensive academic career, she founded the Frederick Douglass Honors Program at Texas Southern University, the precursor to the Thomas F. Freeman Honors College. Dr. Williams was also the first woman to serve as Provost and Vice President for Academic Affairs at Texas Southern University. She also served as the M.A. thesis advisor for Dr. Michon Benson, who went on to earn her PhD from Rice University and serve as the principal of the WALIPP Academy for boys, which operated on the TSU campus from 2010 to 2014.[44] Reverend Jew Don Boney served as a Houston city councilmember for District D from 1995 to 2001, Mayor Protem (1998–2001), and Associate Director of Texas Southern University's Mickey Leland Center on Poverty, Hunger, and World Peace. Borris Miles currently serves as senator for Texas Senate District 13, where Texas Southern University and Wheeler Avenue Baptist Church are located.

Wheeler Avenue's strong commitment to the community emerged out of Lawson's service as chaplain of the Baptist Students Union at Texas Southern University. It was nurtured by Audrey Lawson's commitment to students' spiritual and educational development. By the early 21st century, Bill Lawson was celebrated as a champion of civil rights at Texas Southern University among TSU alumni. Reflecting on Lawson's commitment a half century later, Professor James Douglas, former President of Texas Southern University and Dean of the Thurgood Marshall School of Law, who was a sophomore at TSU in 1963, described Lawson as "the leader of the Civil Rights Movement in Houston". According to Douglas, Lawson "led most of the protests" and "really was the architect of...most of what happened here in Houston,"[45] particularly the integration of the Houston Independent School District.[46] Perhaps because of Lawson's influence and that of other ministers who shied away from protest, Houston did not have "all the riots" and the "physical conflict" associated with "other parts of the country and the segregated South." Their collective position, along with strong condemnation of more violent forms of student protest by local authorities and community members, helped ensure that the civil rights movement in

Houston remained mostly "civil." In 2020, Rice University renamed a portion of the central campus "The Reverend William A. Lawson Grove," where Lawson is honored for "healing the broken" and "brokering peace."[47] Lawson, age 93, at the time of the space's unveiling, visited the monument with his family, including his two daughters, Melanie Lawson, longtime anchor for Channel 13 and Cheryl Lawson, executive director for WALIPP, both of whom embrace their parents' and Wheeler Avenue's commitment to peace and prosperity.

Wheeler Avenue's example and that of Pleasant Hill Baptist Church and Mt. Gilead Baptist Church affirm that Black Baptist church leaders and members in Texas used a variety of means to promote progress in the communities they served. The broad criticism that some churches have received for being accommodationist, otherworldly, or backwards must be understood within the geopolitical environments in which Black churches operated in Texas and throughout the South and continue to operate in less-than-favorable political environments. What is certain is that leaders and members in these particular congregations worked together to create a better world for church members and the communities in which they lived. The institutions and organizations they individually and collectively inspired, created, and managed have born productive fruit over the past 150 years. They will continue to do so as long as subsequent generations of leaders and members remain committed to education, responsive to their respective environments, and ready for productive exchange.

NOTES

1. Eric McDaniel, *Politics in the Pews: The Political Mobilization of Black Churches* (Ann Arbor: University of Michigan Press, 2008).
2. Alwyn Barr, *Black Texans: A History of Negroes in Texas: 1528-1971* (Austin, TX: The Pemberton Press, 1988).
3. Charles E. Hall, "Progress of the Negro in Texas." *US Department of Commerce* (Washington, DC: Bureau of the Census, 1936): 7.
4. Eric McDaniel, *Politics in the Pews*, 20.
5. National Baptist Convention, USA, Inc. *Minutes* (1962): 150–151. http://media2.sbhla.org.s3.amazonaws.com/aaa/nbc/NBC_1962.pdf
6. Morgan Young, "A Look at the Rich History of Fort Worth's First School for Black Students," June 17, 2022. https://www.wfaa.com/article/entertainment/events/juneteenth/history-fort-worth-first-school-for-black-students/287-862c2945-11dc-4dcd-b53f-bf6ad985706c
7. R. T. Tatum, *The Texas Standard, Volume 7, Number 1, April 1933, Periodical* (April 1933) Beaumont, TX. https://texashistory.unt.edu/ark:/67531/metapth193733/ accessed 11 July 2022, University of North Texas Libraries, *The Portal to Texas History*. https://texashistory.unt.edu; crediting Prairie View A&M University.
8. Ibid.

9. Ibid.
10. "About Prairie View." https://www.pvamu.edu/about_pvamu/college-history/
11. Mary Turner Blanche, *The Preparation and Assignments of the Staff of the I. M. Terrell Senior High School, Fort Worth, Texas* (1951). https://digitalcommons. pvamu.edu/pvamu-theses/620
12. "Principals and Presidents." https://www.pvamu.edu/about_pvamu/college-history/principals-and-presidents/
13. "The Prairie View Standard," June 9, 1917. https://digitalcommons.pvamu. edu/cgi/viewcontent.cgi?article=1270&context=pv-newspapers
14. Gayle W. Hanson, "Terrell, Isaiah Milligan [I.M.] (1859–1931)," *Handbook of Texas Online* (Texas State Historical Association, n.d.). https://www.tshaonline.org/handbook/entries/terrell-isaiah-milligan-im accessed 12 September 2023.
15. Freda Washington, "Lee Hayward (Hawood) Simpson: The Fighting Preacher in Jim Crow Houston, 1920–1967," Major Advisor, Merline Pitre, Professor of History (April 4, 2014).
16. "Conroe Normal and Industrial College." https://thc.texas.gov/learn/historic-resources-survey/african-american-travel-guide-survey-project/establishment-hbcus
17. Bernadette Pruitt, *The Other Great Migration: Black Migration to Houston, 1900-1940* (College Station: Texas A & M University Press, 2013): 262.
18. Ibid.
19. Merline Pitre, *In Struggle against Jim Crow: Lulu B. White and the NAACP* (College Station: Texas A & M University Press, 2010).
20. *The Tiger*, Texas Southern University Yearbook (1962): 14. https://digitalscholarship.tsu.edu/cgi/viewcontent.cgi?article=1014&context=yearbook
21. Washington, "Lee Hayward (Hawood) Simpson," 88.
22. Ibid.
23. "Minutes," National Baptist Convention, USA, Inc., (1962): 160–171. http://media2.sbhla.org.s3.amazonaws.com/aaa/nbc/NBC_1962.pdf
24. Southern Baptist Convention Archives Online. http://media2.sbhla.org.s3.amazonaws.com/aaa/nbc/NBC_1962.pdf
25. Kimitris M. Baltrip, "Samuel Nabrit, 98, Scientist and a Pioneer in Education," *The New York Times*, January 6, 2004. https://www.nytimes.com/2004/01/06/us/samuel-nabrit-98-scientist-and-a-pioneer-in-education.html#:~:text=Samuel%20M.,He%20was%2098
26. *The Tiger*, 24. https://digitalscholarship.tsu.edu/cgi/viewcontent.cgi?article=1014&context=yearbook
27. Robert Joseph Taylor, and Linda M. Chatters, "Importance of Religion and Spirituality in the Lives of African Americans, Caribbean Blacks and Non-Hispanic Whites," *The Journal of Negro Education* 79, no. 3 (2010): 280–294. http://www.jstor.org/stable/20798349
28. *The Tiger*, 77. https://digitalscholarship.tsu.edu/cgi/viewcontent.cgi?article=1015&context=yearbook
29. Ibid., 99.
30. Ibid., 207.
31. All Saints Bible College. https://www.allsaintsonline.info/about_history.html

32. *The Tiger*, 1962. Reverend, Augustana Lutheran Church, TSU Yearbook (1962): 50. https://digitalscholarship.tsu.edu/cgi/viewcontent.cgi?article=1 014&context=yearbook

33. *The Tiger*, Baptist Student Union (1962), 157. https://digitalscholarship.tsu. edu/cgi/viewcontent.cgi?article=1014&context=yearbook).

34. Reverend Bill Lawson, "The HistoryMakers A2010.010," interview by Denise Gines, The HistoryMakers Digital Archive. May 11, 2010, Session 1, tape 1, story 7, Reverend Bill Lawson talks about his early education.

35. Reverend Bill Lawson, "The HistoryMakers A2010.010," interview by Denise Gines, The HistoryMakers Digital Archive. May 11, 2010, Session 1, tape 1, story 1, Slating of Reverend Bill Lawson's interview, https://da-thehistory-makers-org.tsu.idm.oclc.org/story/638634;q=william%20bill%20lawson

36. Object Description, Rev. William "Bill" and Audrey Lawson, Correspondence 1952–1954, Volume 1. https://cdm17006.contentdm.oclc.org/digital/collection/lawson/id/16/rec/1

37. "Emmett Till's Death Inspired a Movement." https://nmaahc.si.edu/explore/stories/emmett-tills-death-inspired-movement

38. "Civil Rights Pioneers Visit Martin Luther King Jr. National Memorial Site and Vow to Support Memorial," *New York Amsterdam News (1962–)*, December 11, 2008. http://tsu.idm.oclc.org/login?url=https://www.proquest.com/historical-newspapers/civil-rights-pioneers-visit-martin-luther-king-jr/docview/2663399047/se-2

39. Mark Newman, *Getting Right With God: Southern Baptists and Desegregation, 1945-1995* (Tuscaloosa and London: University of Alabama Press, 2001).

40. "Houston's First Sit-In," Texas Historical Commission, 2009.

41. "Texas Southern University Tiger Walk North Entrance, Spring 2014." https://digitalscholarship.tsu.edu/homepage/3/

42. "History and Mission," Wheeler Avenue Baptist Church. https://wheelerbc.org/about/history-mission

43. "Texas Southern University, A Brief Profile," 2. https://www.tsu.edu/about/administration/institutional-effectiveness/enrollment-data/pdf/historic-factbooks/0610factbook/general-information.pdf

44. Michon Anita Benson, "Being and Becoming in Eden: A Phenomenological Approach to Toni Morrison's *Paradise*," *Theses (Pre-2016)*, (1999): 133. https://digitalscholarship.tsu.edu/pre-2016_theses/133

45. James M. Douglas, "The HistoryMakers A2014.068," interview by Larry Crowe, The HistoryMakers Digital Archive. March 4, 2014. Session 1, tape 4, story 9, James M. Douglas mentions HistoryMakers Bill Lawson and Pluria Marshall, Sr.

46. James M. Douglas, "The HistoryMakers A2014.068," interview by Larry Crowe, The HistoryMakers Digital Archive. March 4, 2014, Session 1, tape 4, story 2, James M. Douglas talks about the movement to integrate schools in Houston, Texas following the leadership of HistoryMaker Reverend Bill Lawson.

47. Katharine Shilcutt, "Rev. William Lawson Visits Namesake Grove at Rice for First Time." https://news.rice.edu/news/2021/rev-william-lawson-visits-namesake-grove-rice-first-time#:~:text=This%20is%20the%20legacy%20Rice,week%20 for%20the%20first%20time accessed 20 September 2023.

REFERENCES

Baltrip, Kimitris M. "Samuel Nabrit, 98, Scientist and a Pioneer in Education," *The New York Times*, 2004, January 6.

Barr, Alwyn. *Black Texans: A History of Negroes in Texas: 1528-1971* (Austin, TX: The Pemberton Press, 1988).

McDaniel, Eric. *Politics in the Pews: The Political Mobilization of Black Churches* (Ann Arbor: University of Michigan Press, 2008).

Newman, Mark. *Getting Right with God: Southern Baptists and Desegregation, 1945-1995* (Tuscaloosa: University of Alabama Press, 2001).

Pitre, Merline. *In Struggle Against Jim Crow: Lulu B. White and the NAACP* (College Station: Texas A & M University Press, 2010).

Pruitt, Bernadette. *The Other Great Migration: Black Migration to Houston, 1900-1940* (College Station: Texas A & M University Press, 2013).

Taylor, Robert Joseph, and Chatters, Linda M. "Importance of Religion and Spirituality in the Lives of African Americans, Caribbean Blacks and Non-Hispanic Whites," *The Journal of Negro Education*, 79, no. 3 (2010): 280–294.

CHAPTER 2

BAYARD RUSTIN: A PARADIGM FOR RETHINKING SEXUALITY AND RELIGION ON HBCU CAMPUSES

Quincy James Rineheart
Payne Theological Seminary, USA

ABSTRACT

While historically Black colleges and universities (HBCU), at least implicitly, have wrestled with the question of Black being and meaning within an anti-Black world, the author of chapter two argues that, for some, the question takes on an added dimension. Borrowing loosely from Du Bois, the author asks "how does it feel to be Black and gay in a country that values neither?" This, according to the author, is a question that both churches and institutions of higher learning have failed to confront in any meaningful way. Yet, using Bayard Rustin, a Queer Quaker and HBCU educated activist, as a paradigm, the author offers a way to rethink sexuality and religion on historically Black colleges and universities campuses and in so doing reimagine curriculum and pedagogy.

Keywords: Black bodies; normative gaze; Queer; civil rights movement; Wilberforce University; heterosexuality

'Saving' Education, pages 29–48
doi:10.1108/978-1-83708-894-220251003

What does it mean to be Black in a society that does not value Black bodies? The question I raise is certainly not new, but it remains a question for scholarly interrogation. In essence, it attends to the now familiar question W. E. B. DuBois raises in his 1903 classic text, *The Souls of Black Folk*,[1] wherein he asks, "How does it feel to be a problem?"[2]

THE DILEMMA OF BLACKNESS

Historically and presently within the white American social structure, Blackness has been linguistically and hermeneutically categorized as problematic—associated with darkness, evil, sinfulness, and criminality, as opposed to whiteness, which is associated with light, goodness, virtue, and purity. The so-called "Hamitic curse" (Genesis 9:18–29) ascribed to the Black descendants of the biblical son of Noah was used historically to justify slavery. In plantation churches, white preachers would instruct the enslaved people that the Holy Bible taught that "Black people deserved to be subjugated as a result of the 'Curse of Ham,' and that 'good slaves' must obey their earthly masters as they did God."[3] Hearing these messages did not sit well with the enslaved people. As a result of these negative sermons preached, many enslaved Blacks created what religious historian Albert Raboteau called the "invisible institution," an underground religious experience where their identities were affirmed, and they were empowered through radical teachings to survive the horrors of the plantation South. To this day, as Thomas Slaughter writes, "Blackness embodies the ostracized. Under the duress of racial domination, I undergo the now familiar two-pronged process of externally imposed inferiorization and subsequent internalization of that inferiority."[4] But what does it mean to be Black and gay in a society that values neither Blackness nor gayness? How does it feel to be doubly problematic? Within Western social thought, African American men and women were always viewed as sexualized beings, considered a site of public consumption for the white gaze. Suppose we understand the contours of Black sexuality and how it intersects historically, theologically, economically, and politically that gave rise to its social constructs. In that case, one must examine how the Black body was seen as a site for white consumption. Within American slave culture, Black bodies were not rendered human beings with agency, and much like Black gay bodies within the Black church, many Black gay people are considered, according to most biblical fundamentalists, "an abomination." The Black gay body in many religious spaces has become a site of theological condemnation. Within many of our Black sacred spaces, the Black gay body, regarding cultural ethicist Victor Anderson, in "The Black Church and the Curious Body of the Black Homosexual," argues, "there is nobody (literally) more contested in Black churches than the curious body of the black homosexual." Anderson is deeply concerned with how Black religious clergy can support civil, human, and political issues but cannot support black gay bodies who attend their spiritual space every Sunday. In many regards, the Black church profits from our talents, gifts, and money, but we are not worthy of affirmation.

The need to control Black bodies, as during slavery, shifted into the nascent, developing, and established Black Church. What the effects of slavery did to Black people is similarly being invoked on the Black gay body within the Black Church. Womanist Theologian Kelly Brown Douglas argues, "While the Black Church and community share the logic of others who denounce homosexuality, their particular history of White racist oppression and sexual exploitation makes Black homophobia appear even more passionate, trenchant, and unyielding."[5] Black bodies are considered chattel, which speaks to the grand narrative of American exceptionalism that deems Black bodies guilty of something.

If Black bodies are seen as problematic from the normative gaze of whiteness, then Black gay bodies are doubly problematic from the normative gaze of heterosexuality. As a result, it appears that Black gay bodies are worthy only of derision in the rhetoric of the Black Church. From the normative gaze of sacramentality, that is, the appreciation of and delight in the diversity of creation from an Augustinian perspective, the mere creation and existence of Black gay bodies has never been a problem. The Christian Church must be positioned to embark upon the journey toward understanding and embracing sexual differences. Unfortunately, (homo)phobia and notions of Black sexuality have paralyzed the Church universally since St. Augustine. Augustine's proclivity with sexuality significantly affected his thoughts on what constitutes a healthy sexual ethic. Augustine's ideology continues to impact substantially theological thinking, particularly in the Right-Wing Conservative Evangelical Christian Movement. During Augustine's childhood, he wrestled with what he was taught concerning sexuality by his mother, Monica, versus what he felt was right. Augustine found himself wrestling with his lustful desires. Although written years later, it shows the Church's complication with addressing lustful desires and degrading sexual desire as evil. Augustine's mother, Monica, was a devout Catholic who believed in strictly rearing her son. With her embedded theology and what it meant to be a "good Christian", she thought of leading by example, i.e., being married, hoping that Augustine would soon convert to Christianity. Due to his mother's leading, Augustine ended up in a relationship, denouncing any other sexual proclivities that might endanger him. He got engaged and disconnected from unhealthy tides that would go against his upbringing. Scholars argue that Augustine soon "saw the light." converted to Catholicism, and developed a life of total celibacy. This is important to note because, in an attempt to follow the "right" way, the Church believes for one to reach "purity in

God," one must deny their sexuality (sexual pleasures) to be "accepted." These types of conversations require a multifaceted approach to healthy discussions around sexuality. For example, throughout The *Confessions*,[6] the language Augustine uses to describe his sexual impulses are "images of disease, disorder, and corruption." For Augustine, one's inability to *not* sin is because one's *desire* to do right is diseased.

Bayard Rustin, much like Augustine, felt that his (homo)sexuality created tension with the folks he was connected to. In letters written to Abraham Johannes (A.J.) Muste, founder of the Fellowship of Reconciliation and mentor to Bayard, Rustin's sexual desires for men were seen as "utterly undisciplined, deceitful, and ruinous to the pacifist cause."[7] Rustin expressed deep remorse to Muste for his actions and wrote, "my weakness and stupidity jeopardized immensely the causes for which…I would be willing to die." Rustin continued by saying, "My behavior stopped progress" and asked that "you and the FOR and all others… forgive me for the damage I have done."[8]

HOW DOES IT FEEL TO BE A PROBLEM?

What can a Civil Rights Movement, Queer Quaker teach us about Historically Black Colleges and Universities (HBCU) culture? How can Black LGBTQ figures inform our pedagogy? Within most HBCU classrooms worldwide, the core curriculum often fails to recognize the lives, contributions, or written texts of Black LGBTQ persons thoroughly and meaningfully.

This essay will provide a historiography of Bayard Rustin as a paradigm or framework for rethinking sexuality and religion on HBCU campuses. Rustin's foundational religious experience, inherited from his Quaker grandmother, reflected a robust social justice gospel emphasizing "intellectual openness, a broad range of doctrinal acceptability, disciplined spirituality, and the peace witness."[9] Although Mrs. Julia Davis Rustin, Rustin's (grand)mother, was Quaker, his (grand)father, Mr. Janifer Rustin, was a member of the African Methodist Episcopal Church. This space exposed Rustin to "African American spirituals and gospel music."[10] The combination was pivotal to Rustin's religious and social justice development. In addition, Rustin attended two HBCUs. Although he did not obtain a formal degree, he studied intermittently at Wilberforce University (an African Methodist Episcopal Church institution), founded in 1856, becoming the first HBCU *owned* and *operated* by Black people. After leaving Wilberforce abruptly, he transferred to Cheyney University of Pennsylvania (a Quaker institution), formally known as Cheyney State Teachers College, another HBCU founded in 1837 as the Institute for Colored Youth.

Mindful of the above, I craft the following argument in three parts. First, I suggest the antigay, antiqueer harms Rustin experienced during the Civil

Rights Movement continue in much the same way Black queer students are excluded from the curricula on HBCU campuses. I want to suggest how DuBois's question helps us think deeply about the educational violence, historical and spiritual suffering inflicted upon the Black Queer body politic that has and continues to be the problem, a form of anthropological and theological terrorism. Lastly and perhaps most generatively, this essay raises the difficult but essential inquiry into how Black queer folks survive when religious or secular institutions de-sacralize their bodies. Is the sacred *always* and *only* heterosexual? How does it feel to be a *spiritual* problem met with theological violence and institutional terror?

Although the Church and HBCUs are sometimes attentive to the issue of anti-blackness and its historical injuries, it often derides heteronormative violence as evidence of its sinful nature. For example, I taught students at Morehouse College who preferred to use pronouns different from their assigned gender identities. One of my students used she/they pronouns to describe themselves. While it was a respected model in my classroom, some of my colleagues refused to address students outside of the hypermasculine traditions and culture of Morehouse College. Students have informed me of certain professors who stated: *This is an all-male school. Why should I be made to refer to students using different pronouns?* The refusal and gender policing of pronouns is nothing more than a form of anti-blackness and anti-gayness that happens far too often within the HBCU culture. HBCUs are critical institutions to higher education, much like Black religion is to church folks. HBCUs have served as protest institutions against segregated Jim Crow. HBCUs have also served as prophetic institutions against the hypocrite of white supremacy. As a graduate of Wilberforce University, I can attest to the sheer power and brilliance of Black intellectual thought being taught in the classroom, which helps to shape the minds of curious students interested in transforming the world. While HBCUs have served as spaces of intellectual transformation, HBCUs have also served as antagonistic spaces for LGBTQ+ students.

And so, this essay proposes a new paradigm to examine violence and trauma more closely to understand how Black queer folk might begin to create sacred worth within contexts marked by ongoing institutionalized discrimination and heteronormative violence against LGBTQ+ folk. This discrimination is undoubtedly true in the exemplary life and work of the Civil Rights icon, strategist, and tactician Bayard Taylor Rustin.

THE BLACK BODY IN THE SLAVOCRACY

The irony is that in the context of the slavocracy, Black bodies never belonged to those who supposedly embodied the putatively negative associations of Blackness. The American slave culture did not render Black bodies as human beings with agency. We must be willing to write a new American history challenging the Anglo-Saxon myth of their superiority, in which Black bodies were then and are still seen as a threat to their persons and to the institutional structures that have been set in place to subjugate and ultimately destroy the Black body politic—civic engagement, individual and corporate morale, mental and physical health, life prospects.

DuBois's provocative question, "How does it feel to be a problem?", points out what pastoral theologian Nicholas Grier posits as "the implications of intersubjectivity for Black people by considering internal feelings in the context of social reality."[11] The DuBoisian framework of "the problem" demonstrates how racism, sexism, and heteronormativity function within the empirical structure. For DuBois, being *a problem* is "a strange experience—peculiar even for one who has never been anything else..."[12] The *problem* that DuBois probes, although in the 1900s, is deeply relevant to Black and Brown men and women who are subjugated and deemed criminal before a verdict is ever rendered.

Rustin, on August 30, 1968, is quoted in the *Miami Times* as saying,

> At a time when America's outstanding problems are poverty, urban decay and racism at home and a tragic and brutal war abroad, the most resounding pledge the Republican Party made to the American people at Miami Beach was to preserve 'law and order'- which as everyone knows, is a pledge to keep the Negro in his place.

In our current context, socio-politically, it is easy for whites to justify the claim of the "problematic" status of Blacks when Black people are killing each other. Such observations pivot away from the problem of Black bodies that are killed without justification through police brutality, medical apartheid, genocide, and the like. In her book, *African Americans and the Culture of Pain*,[13] Debra Walker King posits, "the Black body is always already characterized stereotypically as belonging to the 'brute', a criminal and illegitimate heir of U.S. citizenship whose presence is a national threat."[14] As a result, for instance, Michael Brown, the Ferguson (Missouri) youth gunned down by police officer Darren Wilson, became a national symbol for what happens when the Black body is deemed a defect: the consequence becomes the Black body must be put to death. The fact that Michael Brown's bloody body laid in the hot sun uncovered for 4½ hours discarded by white police officers illustrates the deep problem of racism and white supremacy in the American consciousness. King continues by stating, "by making hurtful stereotypes almost inescapable while also supporting and maintaining an infrastructure of institutionalized racism, body reading stigmatizes black people thoroughly—even jeopardizing the lives of those who are innocent of the stories their bodies tell."[15] Concomitantly, it foregrounds the nature of King's assessment that the Black body is always already criminalized because the police are behaviorally predisposed to shoot first and ask questions later. Similarly, the Atlantic slave trade wounded, maimed and terrorized the bodies of Black individuals and the Black body politic. Womanist Theologian M. Shawn Copeland said, "slavery was social sin: it was moral and physical evil acted out on black bodies."[16] Black bodies were weighed on scales to see if their bodies would bring the master a profit. The Black body politic witnessed it. If Black bodies were not deemed profitable, they were discarded as non-useable, thrown overboard like excess cargo, or left on the ship to keep working. The Black body politic witnessed it. The Black body historically has been seen as a site of terror. Again, the Black body politic witnessed and continues to witness this historical, anthropological, and psychological terrorism. To understand slavery as a social sin for Copeland is to understand how embodied Blackness has always been seen as nonbeing, brute, nothingness, and demonic.

Demonizing the Black body is a notion upheld in many of our churches, for nothing good, according to the Apostle Paul, dwells in the flesh. Many Black churches use this rhetoric to control the Black body, which has been and remains dangerous. In her text, *What's Faith Got to Do With It?*, womanist theologian Kelly Brown Douglass argues that "Platonized Christianity, in essence," helped give rise to the social constructs that impede one understanding of Black sexuality. She claims that "Platonized Christianity sexualizes Christian outsiders." Platonized Christianity is deeply rooted in a white supremacist ideology, supported by Douglass's estimation, "Black people's sexualization and demonization." For Douglass, Platonized Christianity intentionally leaves certain people open for sacrifice. According to the Apostle Paul, this platonic dualism creates notions that "nothing good dwells in the flesh."[17] This dualism further challenges understanding the beauty and celebration of Black sexuality in all its forms. Platonized Christianity was practiced within church culture and demonstrated in the Civil Rights Movement among Black clergypersons.

Why is the conversation on Bayard Rustin so meaningful, one might ask? It is important because: (1) for years, Rustin was hidden in the shadows and given little to no attention for his contributions to society, (2) the humanity and dignity of LGBTQ persons are still rendered invisible and castigated by the church society and classrooms.

WHO WAS BAYARD TAYLOR RUSTIN?

Many are unfamiliar with his story, identity, or historical significance. Those who may be familiar with Rustin automatically raise homosexuality as a primary identifier. Although Rustin was gay, he offered more than his sexuality to the cause of social and political justice. During his memorial service in September of 1987, given by Norman Hill, Rustin's protégé said of him, "for all of us, Bayard Rustin was more than an inspirational leader, a committed activist, an intellectual of uncommon depth and courage. So how does one capture the essence of so unique, complex, and individualistic a person? Are adjectives like principled, outrageous, daring, fearless, loyal, exuberant, vain do him justice?"[18]

He was born March 17, 1912, in West Chester (PA), and was raised by his (grand)parents, Julia and Janifer Rustin. Rustin was born to Florence Rustin (mother) and Archie Hopkins (father), two teenagers who did not have the means to raise a child. Rustin's grandparents became his parents. Julia and Janifer named Rustin after Bayard Taylor, a diplomat, literary critic, and Quaker. Much of Rustin's social activism was learned at the tutelage of his grandmother, whom he loved. Rustin was a precocious child who valued the lessons of liberation and freedom taught by his grandmother. He recalls, "my grandmother was thoroughly convinced that when it came to matters of the liberation of Black people, we had much more to learn from the Jewish experience than we had to learn out of Matthew, Mark, Luke, and John." Those lessons, he continued, "made me extremely militant in terms of achieving things on this earth."[19] Those invaluable lessons taught by his grandmother would ultimately shape who he would become. Bayard, in many ways, was a triple threat. He was a communist until 1941, Gay and Quaker, among other things. Much of his Quaker upbringing was passed down to him from his (grand)mother and her mother, Elizabeth Davis. In addition to being a Quaker, his (grand)mother was one of the first local members of the National Association for the Advancement of Colored People after its founding in 1909. Although he grew up in a household that advocated for both Quaker values from his (grand)mother and African Methodist Episcopal church values from his (grand)father, Rustin continued the Quaker tradition.

It was at Cheyney State that Rustin's intellectual curiosity was formulated and aligned in an official way with his Quaker philosophy. Although many of his Quaker beliefs were instilled in him at an early age, it was a lecture he heard by one of the most respected Quakers, Rufus Matthew Jones, a professor of philosophy at Haverford College, that nurtured his spiritual development forward as "Rustin was, in Quaker fashion, depending upon his daily quiet periods for guidance."[20] German theologian Nicole Hirschfelder, in her book *Oppression as Process: The Case of Bayard Rustin*[21] quotes Rustin as he reflects on his Quakerism: "I think my earliest influences were those of the Quakers, the belief in non-injury, non-violence, respect for other people, and the like."[22] Hence, the Quaker tradition significantly informed the pacifism Rustin used to help Dr. King fundamentally shape the work of the Civil Rights Movement through an adherence to non-violent resistance.

The Quaker tradition (which believes in the dignity of all human worth) significantly informed the pacifism Rustin used to help Dr. King fundamentally shape the work of the Civil Rights Movement into a mode of nonviolent resistance.

Because of his work as an activist, Hirschfelder posits, "Rustin was faced with a high degree of hostility that at times also erupted physical violence."[23] She continues by saying, "according to Quaker values, Rustin instead only 'fought back' with words."[24] Still, it is important to say, the marginality Rustin experienced within/out of the movement, which was Black Church-led in certain respects, was not because he was Quaker but because he was a part of the Young Communist League (up until 1941) and gay. Rustin grew up during the McCarthy (Former US Senator Joseph McCarthy of Wisconsin) era, which opposed anyone who was communist and gay. To be communist and gay (and Black) was antithetical to the cultural norms of mainstream society. Rustin's homosexuality exiled him over time from the memory of people within the Civil Rights Movement. For Rustin, his Black gay body became a site of terror the day he renounced his affiliation with the Civil Rights Movement. According to David McReynolds,[25] he did this because Reverend Adam Clayton Powell Jr., then US Congressman and Senior Pastor of Abyssinian Baptist Church (NYC) threatened Reverend Dr. Martin Luther King, Jr. with false accusations alleging that he and Rustin were involved in a homosexual relationship. Powell demanded that Rustin be relieved of his duties.[26] Until this point, Rustin had assisted the movement in many ways, such as developing the Montgomery Bus Boycott, providing training to leaders, tutoring Dr. King in the principles of Gandhian nonviolence philosophy, and drafting speeches for Dr. King. Rustin's Black gay body was not only a "site of trauma" but also made to represent a site of public terror. Rustin's identity threatened the Movement's political, social, and ecclesial "order." Rustin became, for example, a model of what happens when Black gay bodies are antithetical to the social, cultural, and ecclesiastical structures they navigate.

As a Black gay Quaker, Rustin experienced this marginality personally. Yet, before Powell's threat, he orchestrated one of the most influential movements in American History, the historic 1963 March on Washington for Jobs and Freedom. Asa Philip Randolph, a labor unionist, activist, organizer of the brotherhood Sleeping Car Porters, and mentor to Rustin, was responsible for Rustin becoming the face of the 1963 march. Although the march featured Dr. King prominently, as the leader of the Civil Rights Movement, it nevertheless provided Rustin with a platform he used as a tool for transformative leadership. Rustin's lived experience and reflection function as a framework to further understand and empathize with oppressed and alienated persons. Black gay bodies are continually used as sites of terror and exiled because of their sexual orientation.

THE BLACK GAY BODY AS A SITE OF RELIGIOUS TERRORISM

In what other ways have Black Queer bodies become sites of terror? In his essay, "Theorizing the 'Black Body' as a Site of Trauma: Implications for Theologies of Embodiment,"[27] Darnell Moore opens by queering the Black body in three distinct ways: "(1) Bodies speak. (2) Bodies emote. (3) Bodies remember."[28] For Moore, historically, these distinctions become essential to problematize how the "Black body" has always been viewed negatively. Moore states that he is interested in how one can "theorize, or undertheorize, the 'Black body' and the ways the 'black body' can be symbolized as a semiotic figuration of both pain and pleasure and as a site of trauma and grace."[29] Moore further is interested in "theorizing the 'Black body' as a figure located at different historicized scenes and how these 'sightings' ostensibly quicken traumatic memories and memorialize the body as a site of trauma."[30] While I accept Moore's critique that the "Black body" serves as a type of historical marker as a site of trauma, I want to also advance Moore's argument and add that Black Queer bodies serve not only as "sites of trauma" but also as sites of terror, often the by-product of prolonged trauma. This is to suggest that terrorism is the act itself, while trauma produces the after-effects, which create other sites of terror, evoking unrelenting, "cascading" violence.[31]

In defining Black gay bodies as sites of terrorism, I illustrate how pain is imposed upon the body from external forces that view the Black gay body politic as a "threat" or "threatening danger" to the established culture. In his book, *Terror and Triumph: The Nature of Black Religion*, humanist scholar Anthony Pinn, a professor at Rice University, examines how enslaved Black bodies became constructed sites of terror. He writes that this terror results from how the auction block strips away early self-perceptions and meaning, imposing in their place "otherness" and historical irrelevance. Dread or terror in this sense is profound in that it forces the enslaved person to confront their helplessness, isolation from the familiar, and submersion in absurdity.[32] Following Pinn's lead, I argue that Rustin's Black gay body, in its queer performativity, functioned as a 20th-century example of domestic and religious terrorism produced in the wake of the auction block and as an effect of its afterlife. While we are unclear about the psychological trauma Rustin experienced, one can imagine the pain of being rejected for living in their truth. Indeed, we see how similar terror is invoked on Black gay bodies daily, specifically in the Black Church during the sermon, for example. As in Rustin's case, Black gay bodies are regularly pimped for their talents but denigrated for their existence.

During the 107th Holy Convocation of the Church of God in Christ, in Saint Louis (MO), November 3–11, 2014, former Superintendent Earl Carter—one of the high-ranking elders (i.e., clergy persons) in his denomination—delivered an evening message entitled "Church, Come Out of Sin." As he preached about "sin," Elder Carter wanted to know "why people kept sinning?" He went on to state the reason(s) why he thought people "keep sinning," which was "they don't want to be delivered." As he preached, he made an abrupt turn in the message, which illustrates how the Black gay body became a site of religious terror. He states, and I quote him at length (this language may be triggering for some, but try to bear with me):

> I got something for all of you. I got something for all these homosexuals who are switching, carryin' purses, wearing your bow-ties, wearing your tight pants, looking like a girl...I got the answer... You, homosexuals, need deliverance! Imma tell you why you aren't delivered, and Imma tell you what's wrong with you! Walking around here lookin' like a sissy. You are perverted, and you are lost. You're walking like a woman...you are a highly conundrum; you're a confusion. That's okay; nobody wants to tell these homosexuals they're living in sin, but Imma tell them because homosexuals don't want to hear the truth. You want to feel like a girl? I wish that God will give you the month of a girl. I wish God will have you bleeding out of your butt since you want to be a girl. God should put it all on you because the homosexual is the punishment.[33]

In his violent sermon, Elder Carter's homophobic and terroristic rhetoric points further to how Black gay bodies continue to exist as sites of theological terrorism. This is precisely the opposite of the definition of love and care, and so the Black Church has alternately failed to preach the good news of redemption regarding its LGBTQIA and non-gender-conforming members. The quest to be accepted and affirmed as a source of validation from the Black Church places the onus on Black gay bodies to stay in their place. Such repression of their physicality continues to threaten the well-being of who they are at their core. Against the religious and theological framework surrounding the Black body, the Black queer body experiences heightened terrorism from within and without its cultural milieu.

There are strong similarities between the articulation of an anti-gay stance within the church setting (which uses theology as a weapon) and curriculum in the classroom that excludes LGBTQ+ folk. In his critical text, *Black and Queer on Campus*, anthropologist Michael P. Jeffries conducted an ethnographic study of what life is like for LGBTQ+ students. He posits, "research shows that LGBTQ+ college students of all backgrounds and at all types of schools suffer mistreatment in class. They may feel silenced during class discussion, rendered invisible by the material covered in their courses, and have trouble forming strong relationships with their instructors."[34] As the former Associate Campus Minister and Adjunct Professor of Africana Studies at Morehouse College, this matter hits on a personal level. An example of this form of exclusion as violence was experienced by Black queer students at Morehouse College when the Rustin Crown Forum lecture by Marlon Bailey (Professor of Gender and Sexuality and Women Studies at Arizona State University) was removed by the College's Administration because it, students were told, was deemed "too sexually explicit and could potentially hurt the fund-raising efforts of the president." My former student, Morehouse alumnus Christian Taylor, a gender-fluid young person, recounts their experience in a letter proposed to the administration, which I share in length to demonstrate this form of violence perpetuated by HBCU Administration:

On March 17th, 2022, Morehouse College held its annual Bayard Rustin Crown Forum, which is a Crown Forum that intends to focus on the experiences, lives, and existences of the Black queer community at the college and globally. 2022's Bayard Rustin Crown forum was incredibly monumental because it revealed the portrait unveiling introduction of Dr. Pauli Murray—a gender-nonconforming individual—to the African American Hall of Fame. The introduction of any portrait, especially the first queer figure, is monumental and one to praise. The festive celebration further escalated with the renowned Arizona State University professor researching Black (gay) Men, Dr. Marlon Bailey.

Dr. Bailey's lecture was similar to his previous one at Emory, sponsored by Spelman College, which you can still find on Youtube today. This lecture described the "cum busting on ass and squirting out of holes" that occurred at underground gay sex parties. These words existed uncensored to show the Black men's pleasurable, erotic, authentic experience, telling themselves and the world that they are justified and valid in their existence. However, Morehouse delegitimized gay people's existence, voices, and lives when the institution censored Dr. Bailey's lecture. The potential Black gay men who walk through Morehouse's doors and engage in these actions will now feel seen within the world or collegiate community. They must sit through lectures and discussions that suggest heterosexuality through biological talks, Brown Street discussions, NSO (New Student Orientation) events, and other Crown Forums. Thus, the one lecture that could have represented their experience, or was approximate to it, is now wholly reinforced with aggressive heterosexuality that supersedes unabated. Therefore, the real Morehouse Black Men's Study suggests the study of the restricted and one-dimensional (Cisgender) heterosexual Black men's experiences. The aforementioned realization leads one to ask: how does Morehouse reconcile its proclaimed mission within the Black Men's Research Institute and the institutional organization that presents itself as the antithesis of that? Heteronormativity infected us, giving us damaged eyesight about how we see Sexuality, sex, and gender. I propose

Morehouse address their paradoxical nature as one would a virus since heteronormativity acts like a contagion.[35]

Taylor's proposed letter and critical questions to the administration point out the heteronormativity continually perpetuated in HBCU academic spaces such as Morehouse College. Some may ask, why wasn't this letter sent? Why is this coming out now? While all conjecture can be discussed, it is clear what happens when folks buck against the Empire. To be clear, I am not positioning Morehouse College as a lousy institution; I love and respect the institution dearly. However, I want to point to how institutionalized power (i.e., higher administration) determines what is deemed appropriate and what is considered offensive. The purpose for receiving a Liberal Arts education is to be open to learning and to be challenged to think differently and more expansively and this would include *raw* and uncomfortable material being taught.

In his essay entitled, "The Man's Man: Shame and the African American Male," Biko Gray critiques the unyielding nature of Black masculinity, generally denoted in the Black Church and communities as exclusively heterosexual, void of any customarily female-gendered experiences such as valuing and expressing emotions, avoiding any preening behavior, dominant in his household, social and ecclesiastical circles, overtly, internally, and vigilantly hyper-masculine. Gray queries: What makes a man? The Black community in America is particularly rigid in how it presents and preserves the African-American male. Mainstream African American culture (including some forms of Black religion) displays the Black male as "hard"; the Black male should be insensitive, defensive, and sometimes even belligerent. He should be the "breadwinner," making money for the family while the woman is at home with the kids. He should play sports, but he should not want to dance. He should want to hang out with other males and participate in the unfolding misogyny. And, most of all, he cannot be homosexual. "Fags" are not men. Gray examines the interlocking nature of the oppressive rhetoric of homophobia consistently present in mainstream society. I grew up hearing, internalizing, and struggling with the biblically based homophobic discourse, which stated that "homosexuality is an abomination," that it was a "White thing," and that "Africa did not have homosexuals before Europeans went there." I always find the statement about "Adam and Steve" versus "Adam and Eve" particularly irksome since the Church quickly affirmed that we are all children of God. The most liberal thing I heard about homosexuality growing up as a Black Baptist was, "Hate the sin; love the sinner," which is both ontologically problematic and theologically impossible.[36] In the article, "Like a Voice Crying in the Wilderness: Preaching and Professing a Sexual Discourse of Resistance from the Outside in the Black Church," Gary L. Lemons argues persuasively against the moral posture of the rhetoric "hate the sin, love the sinner."

He posits "that such rhetoric is rooted in self-righteous doctrinal legalism, mean-spirited heterosexist anxiety, and fear—commingled with callous and venomous homophobia." Sadly, the Church is only willing to love whom-ever it can benefit from—whether they are "in sin" or not. It does not "hate" the sin and "love" the sinner. The Church often hates the sin and the sinner or tolerates the sin and the sinner if the sinner's gifts can be used unto their glory.[37]

The myopic attitude of many in Black churches and institutions that con-demn homosexuality or police sexual expression significantly hinders the ecumenical churches or institutional ability to conduct a healthy dialog. This position causes many to wonder why the Church is even being asked to respond to this "epidemic" of homosexuality when those who are members of the LGBTQ community "willingly live in sin." Further, as an institution committed primarily to patriarchy, the Black Church is often unsympathetic to homosexuality because this orientation does not perpetuate male domi-nance over women—the cornerstone of the Black Church structure. There-fore, since homosexuality seemingly adds nothing to the life and structure of the Church, many cannot see how healthy dialog around homosexuality is beneficial to the Church's future. Most churches would instead dissolve the issue of homosexuality altogether. Yet, since they cannot eliminate it, they tolerate the "sin" and give little attention to whatever ills it might be presumed to engender.

While Rustin did not experience harsh treatment from his family, he certainly understood what it meant to be objectified and nullified by those he considered supporters, who were significant operatives within the Black Church. Nevertheless, Rustin becomes an exemplar of what it means to be exiled because of one's sexual orientation and for Black gay bodies to cre-ate sacred worth.

THE BLACK GAY BODY AND EXILE

Historically, exile has been understood as estrangement, which creates, in many ways, the possibility of return. In the case of Black gay bodies in exile, I ask, to whom are we returning? Alternatively, how can exile be a site of religious resistance against the historical milieu and current context? In this section, I want to problematize this concept of exile not as a point of return but as a springboard for Black gay bodies to go forth and create sacred worth. In effect, exile, in many cases, may be necessary to engender holistic and transformative living.

In order for Black gay bodies to create sacred value and meaning in the world and the Church, Black gay bodies will have to free themselves from the religious dogma and theological toxicity that has terrorized and demonized their existence. For some, this may mean leaving homophobic churches and institutions for affirming ones. For some, this may mean staying in these churches and institutions while calling them toward greater recognition. For some, it may mean creating new places and spaces of salvation, redemption, and wholeness beyond traditional church settings. Bayard Rustin was indeed a model for radical and transformative leadership. Rustin's life and witness exemplify what it means to create sacred worth.

Although Rustin, on many occasions, wrote for King, tutored King in nonviolent conflict, introduced him to Gandhian philosophy, played a crucial role in the Montgomery bus boycott, and orchestrated one of the nation's most potent marches, the 1963 March on Washington for Jobs and Freedom, he has been a footnote in the memories of the movement for some people. Yet, in the final decades of Rustin's life, he created a sacred space for himself, filled with meaning and purpose. Rustin worked very diligently to end apartheid in South Africa, but most importantly, Rustin found personal peace. Rustin, in 1977, began a longstanding relationship with Walter Nagele, his partner, who currently resides in New York City. According to Walter, Rustin was never one to speak about his private life. However, Rustin said,

> The most important thing is that after many years of seeking, I've finally found a solid, ongoing relationship with one individual with whom I have everything in common, everything...I spent years looking for exciting sex instead of looking for a compatible person.[38]

Much of the 1960s Civil Rights Movement, in many regards, is the philosophical and political imagination of Rustin being performed in the public square.

Rustin was more than a gay man; he was a global cosmopolitan who championed the "least of these." Rustin often reminded us, "the only weapon we have is our bodies, and we need to tuck them in places, so wheels don't turn." Personal peace is the benchmark of a faithful person. In his exilic spatiality, Rustin effectuated lasting change. His peace-making, over time, has given rise to a public affirmation of his sacred worth. It is most evident in the posthumous Presidential Medal of Freedom award conferred by President Barack Obama in 2013. Rustin exemplifies for Black queer and gender non-conforming folks that our reality has sacred worth. In order for Black gay bodies to create sacred value and meaning in the world and the church, Black gay bodies will have to free themselves from the religious dogma that has terrorized and demonized their existence. For some, this may mean leaving homophobic churches for affirming ones. For some, this may mean staying in these churches while calling them toward greater recognition. For some, it means advocating for LGBTQ+ professors and classes to be taught. For some, it may mean creating new places and spaces of salvation, redemption, and wholeness beyond traditional church settings.

A BLACK QUEER CURRICULUM PARADIGM AT MOREHOUSE

In the Fall semester of 2022, Morehouse College received a $4,000 grant through what was formally known as Interfaith Youth Core (now Interfaith America) to address a severe health crisis, namely HIV/AIDS, which disproportionally affects African Americans in the South. In a world reeling from escalating demonization of sexuality in American Culture, divisive political rhetoric that aims to divide the nation on ideals of love, justice, and the pursuit of happiness, and an epidemic of religious and institutional terrorism that seeks to eradicate the rights of queer and trans persons from living their authentic lives, HBCUs must do "the work their soul must-have," to quote the late Dr. Katie Geneva Cannon. Part of developing this paradigm involves the classroom. So, what does this mean for many of our HBCUs with large populations of LGBTQ+ students on campus?

It means that HBCUs must be willing to create a critical pedagogical intervention that is cutting-edge, inclusive, and reflected in the larger mission statement. Rustin is vital here because the Rustin Crown Forum, named in his honor, is for Morehouse's LGBTQ+ students. Upon receiving the $4,000 grant, I proposed a project to focus on developing a Black Queer Curriculum that addresses HIV/AIDS and faith on HBCU College campuses. Within most HBCU classrooms, the core curriculum does not often recognize the lives, contributions, or written texts of Black LGBTQIA persons. One student said, "Professor Rineheart, your class is the first class I have taken in four years where I see myself in the text." Related to this, while conducting his research, one of Professor Jeffries's interviewees discussed the importance of seeing himself in the material. He states, "I don't see myself in my professors and classes. Like they're mostly like cis straight people and like, I don't know, I just, I don't ever feel like I connect with them, besides going to class and leaving and doing my homework."[39] This is important because transformational teaching ensures that professors provide students with texts that allow them to see themselves.

This Black Queer Curriculum I proposed would address the following: (1) strategies for tackling the HIV/AIDS epidemic among HBCU campuses, (2) ways to discuss a discourse that addresses a healthy sexual ethic that does not demonize the body but appreciates the fullness of one's sensuality and spirituality, (3) a discourse for how the Black Queer curriculum can implement strategies that are praxis orientated toward building inclusive classrooms for those students who are members of the LGBTQIA community, and lastly (4) how the Black Queer curriculum can be presented to faculty, staff, and administration to be instituted in the mission statement of the college and pedagogy. The challenge is to engage in critical self-reflection that requires Black Christians sitting with the incarnated Christ—i.e., the center of the Black Church and Christian faith to dismantle embedded ideologies and phobias that seek to divide us; to be the balm in Gilead where those who are wounded can experience healing and wholeness; to create religious and social policies that provide sustainable outcomes for the marginalized; to educate against ignorance that seeks to blinded us to the truth of new possibilities; and to be a caring community that loves people into their liberation.

In the Spring of 2022, I taught "Introduction to Gender and Sexuality Studies," the fourth course ever offered in the history of the college related to the topic. We used an interdisciplinary approach. We examined the historical, theoretical, and conceptual frameworks for understanding health (HIV/AIDS), sex, law, politics, race, economics, class, and religion through a Black feminist gaze. We explored questions such as: What is Gender? What is Sexuality? Is Gender Fluid? Is Sexuality static? What does it mean to express queer, trans, and non-gender conforming expressions of the self? How do gender, sex, and sexuality impact how we understand the intersecting systems of oppression, such as racism, sexism, homophobia, transphobia, and ableism? We also explored contemporary figures such as Lil Nas X, Dwayne Wade, Willow Smith, and Zaya Wade to explore how the way each performed gender in the public square disrupts and deconstructs heteronormative gender roles.

In the Fall of 2022, I taught a course titled "Black Queer Peace Activists: Pauli Murray and Bayard Rustin." This course explores the powerful legacies of these two figures. Both were radical revolutionaries, politically astute peace activists, moral cosmopolitans, and strategic organizers whose influence extended far beyond the Civil Rights Movement. With close examination, much of their lives intersected. Both were born and died two years apart. Both were raised by their (grand)parents/aunts. Both were part of a religious institution (Murray, an Episcopalian, and Rustin, a Quaker). Both were queer and exiled to the margins because of their sexuality. We examine the convergences and confluences of these two figures' political and social ideologies—and the worlds that shaped them. We explored their queerness, international and foreign connections, public and social policies, spirituality, and activism that shaped the moral consciousness of the United States of America. We paid special attention to both primary and secondary sources as a window into contemporary debates about intersubjectivity as experienced in African American culture that gives rise to the notion of a collective self (or a collective we), the hallmark of the African American experience. This class is grounded in the Black radical tradition and speaks to the Black queer presence and the importance of peace activism as a form of resistance. From Bayard Rustin to Black trans- and non-gendered folks, Black LGBTQ+ people have always and will forever be vital to the movement of Black liberation.

NOTES

1. W. E. B. DuBois, *The Souls of Black Folk* (New York: Penguin Books, 1903).
2. Ibid., 3.
3. Juan M. Floyd-Thomas, *Liberating Black Church History: Making It Plain* (Nashville, TN: Abingdon Press, 2014): 48.
4. Cited in George Yancy, *Black Bodies, White Gazes: The Continuing Significance of Race* (New York: Rowman & Littlefield, 2008).
5. Kelly Brown Douglas, *Sexuality and the Black Church: A Womanist Perspective* (Maryknoll, NY:Orbis Books, 1999): 89.
6. St. Augustine, *Saint Augustine Confessions: A New Translation by Henry Chadwick* (Oxford: Oxford World's Classics; Oxford University Press, 2009).
7. John D'Emilio, *Lost Prophet: The Life and Times of Bayard Rustin* (New York: Free Press, 2003): 102, 114–115.
8. Ibid., 104, 113.
9. Profile of Bayard Rustin by Michael Westmoreland-White, August 4, 2003.
10. Harold Weaver, Paul Kriese, and Stephen W. Angell, *Black Fire: African American Quakers on Spirituality and Human Rights* (Philadelphia, PA: Quaker Press of Friends General Conference, 2011): 151.
11. Nicholas Grier, *Care for the Mental and Spiritual Health of Black Men: Hope to Keep Going* (Lanham, MD: Lexington Books, 2020): 53.
12. DuBois, *Souls of Black Folk*, 75.
13. Debra Walker King, *African Americans and the Culture of Pain* (Charlottesville: University of Virginia Press, 2008).
14. Ibid., 13.
15. Ibid., 12.
16. M. Shawn Copeland, *Enfleshing Freedom: Body, Race, and Being* (Minneapolis, MN: Fortress Press, 2010): 116.
17. See Brown Douglass, *What's Faith Got to Do With It?*, 3–39.
18. Norman Hill, *The Eulogy of Bayard Taylor Rustin* (Unpublished). 1987.
19. D'Emilio, *Lost Prophet*, 11–12.
20. Ibid., 26.
21. Nicole Hirschfelder, *Oppression as Process: The Case of Bayard Rustin* (Heidelberg: Universitatsverlag Winter Heidelberg, 2014): 139.
22. Ibid., 139.
23. Ibid., 139.
24. Ibid., 139.
25. John D'Emilio, "Troubles I've Seen: Rustin and the Price of Being Gay", in *Bayard Rustin: A Legacy of Protest and Politics* (New York: New York University Press, 2023): 139.
26. D'Emilio, *Lost Prophet*, 195.
27. Darnell Moore, "Theorizing the 'Black Body' as a Site of Trauma: Implications for Theologies of Embodiment", *Theology & Sexuality*, 15, no. 2 (2015, April 21): 175–188
28. Ibid., 177.
29. Ibid., 178.
30. Ibid., 179.
31. Foster Marsha Boyd, "Covenant Care and Cascading Violence". Delivered at Chicago Theological Seminary, October 13, 2016.

32. Anthony Pinn, *Terror and Triumph: The Nature of Black Religion* (Minneapolis, MN: Augsburg Fortress Publishers, 2003).
33. Earl Carter, The Sermon Delivered During the 107th Holy Convocation of the Church of God in Christ in Saint Louis, MO (November 3–11, 2014).
34. Michael P. Jeffries, *Black and Queer on Campus* (New York: New York University Press, 2023): 160.
35. Christian Taylor, *An Open Letter to Morehouse College* (never submitted, but used with his permission), March 17, 2022.
36. Biko Gray, "The Man's Man: Shame and the African American Male". Unpublished paper, 2010: 1.
37. See Gary L. Lemons, "Like a Voice Crying in the Wilderness: Preaching and Professing 'a Sexual Discourse of Resistance' From the Outside in the Black Church," in *Facilitating Campus Climates of Pluralism, Inclusion and Progressive Change at HBCUs*, eds. M. Jacqui Alexander and Beverly Guy-Sheftall (Atlanta, GA: Women's Research & Resource Center, Spelman College, 2011), 73–97.
38. David Brooks, *The Road to Character* (New York: Random House, 2015): 151.
39. Jeffries, *Black and Queer on Campus*, 160.

REFERENCES

Augustine. *Saint Augustine Confessions: A New Translation by Henry Chadwick* (Oxford: Oxford World's Classics; Oxford University Press, 2009).

Brooks, David. *The Road to Character* (New York: Random House, 2015).

Copeland, M. Shawn. *Enfleshing Freedom: Body, Race, and Being* (Minneapolis, MN: Fortress Press, 2010).

DuBois, W. E. B., *The Souls of Black Folk* (New York: Penguin Books, 1903).

D'Emilio, John. "Troubles I've Seen: Rustin and the Price of Being Gay", in *Bayard Rustin: A Legacy of Protest and Politics* (New York: New York University Press, 2023).

D'Emilio, John. *Lost Prophet: The Life and Times of Bayard Rustin* (New York: Free Press, 2003).

Douglas, Kelly Brown. *Sexuality and the Black Church: A Womanist Perspective* (Maryknoll, NY: Orbis Books, 1999).

Floyd-Thomas, Juan M. *Liberating Black Church History: Making It Plain* (Nashville, TN: Abingdon Press, 2014).

Grier, Nicholas. *Care for the Mental and Spiritual Health of Black Men: Hope to Keep Going* (Lanham, MD: Lexington Books, 2020).

Hirschfelder, Nicole. *Oppression as Process: The Case of Bayard Rustin* (Heidelberg: Universitatsverlag Winter Heidelberg, 2014).

Jeffries, Michael P. *Black and Queer on Campus* (New York: New York University Press, 2023).

King, Debra Walker. *African Americans and the Culture of Pain* (Charlottesville: University of Virginia Press, 2008).

Lemons, Gary L. "Like a Voice Crying in the Wilderness: Preaching and Professing 'a Sexual Discourse of Resistance' From the Outside in the Black Church," In *Facilitating Campus Climates of Pluralism, Inclusion and Progressive Change at HBCUs*, edited by M. Jacqui Alexander and Beverly Guy-Sheftall. 73–97. Atlanta, GA: Women's Research & Resource Center, Spelman College, 2011.

Moore, Darnell. "Theorizing the 'Black Body' as a Site of Trauma: Implications for Theologies of Embodiment", *Theology & Sexuality*, 15, no. 2 (2015, April 21): 175–188.

Pinn, Anthony. *Terror and Triumph: The Nature of Black Religion* (Minneapolis, MN: Fortress Press, 2003).

Weaver, Harold, Kriese, Paul, and Angell, Stephen W. *Black Fire: African American Quakers on Spirituality and Human Rights* (Philadelphia, PA: Quaker Press of Friends General Conference, 2011).

Yancy, George. *Black Bodies, White Gazes: The Continuing Significance of Race* (New York: Rowman & Littlefield, 2008).

CHAPTER 3

BLACK RELIGION AND THE SOUL STRUGGLES OF HBCUs

Cleve V. Tinsley
Virginia Union University, USA

ABSTRACT

In this essay, the author maintains a concern with the manner in which the relationship between religion and higher education in the historically Black colleges and universities (HBCU) context has consequences for the inner-person—for a sense of identity and life meaning. However, rather than reading this struggle through an individual, the author offers a general theorization of and attention to the "soul," or what might be named the Black psyche. By means of this conceptual framework and mindful of the religious dimensions of these institutions, the author examines the signs, symbols, and rituals present on HBCU campuses for the ways in which they impact and help to form inner meaning, individual identity, and communal connections.

Keywords: Black psyche; soul; discrimination; "spiritual striving"; anti-blackness; Black soul struggle

This, then, is the end of his striving: to be a co-worker in the kingdom of culture, to escape both death and isolation, to husband and use his best powers and his latent genius. —W. E. B. DuBois[1]

Signifying is a very clever language game, and one has to be adept in the verbal arts either to signify or to keep from being signified upon. —Charles Long[2]

'Saving' Education, pages 49–73
Copyright © 2025 by Emerald Publishing Limited
All rights of reproduction in any form reserved.
doi:10.1108/978-1-83708-894-220251004

The relationship between African-American religion and historically Black colleges and universities (HBCUs) is an intriguing topic to explore,[3] especially given the proliferation of HBCUs after the Civil War when a host of religious leaders, Christian missionaries, and philanthropists descended across the American South to establish institutions for the education of newly emancipated Blacks.[4] Moreover, those conversant with African American religious expression—with Black Churches, especially—and spend time on HBCU campuses might notice a palpable cultural and spiritual resonance operative among its constituents.[5]

Based on shared sets of values, HBCUs express creative and powerful communal ideas, symbols, rituals, and pronouncements that build and sustain social cohesion in ways that have been known as a distinguishing characteristic in the spirituality of African peoples.[6] Furthermore, given how religion has always figured prominently in the lives of African Americans—e.g., African Americans are overrepresented in Black Protestant Christian traditions[7]—expressions of deep cultural (spiritual) kinship resonance should not be all that surprising. Like Black churches, HBCUs have been significant social institutions in African Americans' lives adding in the development for self-expression, shaping racial solidarity and identity, and training future Black leaders.[8] HBCUs are not Black Churches, however. Therefore, how might one interpret and put forth the peculiar *religious* significance of these institutions for young Black Americans today? This is the topic with which this essay is concerned.

I argue that HBCUs are engaged in a perpetual religious struggle, what I call—borrowing from W. E. B. DuBois and a range of other thinkers in African American religious thought—*Black soul struggles*. HBCU Black soul struggles are ongoing collective battles to shape healthy young African American psyches and placements. HBCUs are constantly challenged in their mission to form vigorous senses of Black racial consciousness that aid future African American community, political, and thought leaders' stability and identity as they prepare to enter new social worlds that will always and already be proscribed by the structural disadvantages and societal injustices that attend Black life in America.

Developing young African Americans' sturdy psyches (or souls) and representative bearings has been part of the HBCU mission. Against the backdrop of over 300 years of slavery and a century of racial segregation and discrimination, HBCUs have always had to take on adaptive and expressive functions in the African-American community; they have had to nurture modes of Black cultural orientation and representation that permitted more social mobility and belonging in white-dominant society while simultaneously being concerned with providing safe space for more uninhibited African-American self-expression.

There has been much discourse in recent years about the need for Black churches to respond to and address evolving moral obligations and demands placed on them by ever-changing African-American sociopoliti-cal landscapes.[9] In the same vein, today's HBCUs bear the responsibility of constant introspection and adaptation, ensuring that they recalibrate approaches to provide top-notch education while fostering the personal and leadership development needed for tomorrow's world. African-American communities are witnessing unprecedented perspectives regard-ing the best values, conventions, and methods for participating in the modern American democratic narrative. Many HBCU students are all too familiar with the increasingly daunting challenges to African American life options. Coming out of isolation during a global pandemic only exacer-bated and brought heightened attention to some of the permanent dis-parities African Americans face daily along a range of concerns—such as access to healthcare, police surveillance, and an irretrievable wealth gap.[10] These disparities make it crucial for HBCUs to fulfill what I take to be their religious mission: the cultivation of a healthy sense of identity and Black consciousness for its students in ways that make them conscientious citizens and formidable moral agents in their communities.

ON DUBOIS' SPIRITUAL STRIVING AND THE MEANING AND NATURE OF BLACK SOUL STRUGGLES

My thoughts on Black soul struggles follows the prominent cultural histo-rian and intellectual W. E. B. Du Bois, whose influential *The Souls of Black Folk*[11] elucidates African American travail at the turn of the 20th century. Most are familiar with his notion of "double consciousness" and the sym-bol of the "Veil." They've been steady representations that depict the inner turmoil and sense of boundary work associated with what he saw as a sin-gular kind of "spiritual striving" by African Americans. This striving was for individual and collective senses of fulfillment and contentment by Afri-can Americans—a fight for due recognition, equal participation, and fair structural conditions as Black folks within a newer white post-Emancipation social and political order in the United States.[12]

Double consciousness, for DuBois, refers to how African Americans grapple internally and externally with their sense of American identity. It is a duality that creates constant tension and struggle in Black communi-ties as individuals strive to reconcile their sense of self with the external expectations and stereotypes placed upon them by white-dominant power arrangements. "The Veil," then, can be thought of as a kind of separator, a boundary behind which African Americans might experience some sense of social and psychic safety and concealment from the white normative gazes and strictures that always seem profound on the other side.

As the epigraph above suggests, DuBois saw African Americans as coworkers of creative cultural production, despite the unjust weight of white normativity. He stresses that African Americans have never been passive recipients of culture, but rather active contributors to this nation's artistic, intellectual, and cultural development. He believes that African-American genius and creativity are essential to both the growth and progress of the US.

As a collection of essays, *Souls* has influenced African-American cultural and critical religious thought for some time.[13] And in essays, such as "Of the Faith of Our Fathers" and "Of Our Spiritual Strivings," DuBois still provides enduring heuristics for those wanting to grapple with the complexity of understanding the meaning and nature of African American religious struggle today, a task particularly challenging due to the rather diverse socioeconomic, historical, geographic, and other more personal factors that complicate neat descriptions of how African Americans express their deepest longings for meaning and belonging. As an example, in "Of the Faith of Our Fathers," Du Bois, early on, explores the African-American Christian tradition from a sociocultural perspective, acknowledging the rich and varied religious practices that have emerged within Black Protestantism. He depicts African-American ingenuity here by disclosing how African, European, and American religious traditions have all influenced Black Christianity.[14] Similarly, in "Of Our Spiritual Strivings," Du Bois delves into a distinct complexity when interpreting an African American spirituality vis-à-vis the quest for self-realization, identity and belonging as a deep-seated concern. Here, is where he discusses the famous concept of double consciousness, that sense of being both Black and American and how this duality shapes African Americans' spiritual and existential struggles.[15]

Du Boisian thought remains commendable for religion studies, as he points toward acknowledging the diversity and intricacy within Black religious expression and struggle. Being attuned to such intricacy pushes one to think about the kinds of nuanced approaches that might be necessary to comprehend Black religious expression and struggle. As I'll point out, there are some limitations that may "color," so to speak, and date Du Bois's analyses. Nonetheless, most would agree with a point DuBois makes poignantly clear: the persistent problem of "the color line" remains, and it obstinately fights to secure its borders. Thus, any consideration of what I call *the Black soul struggle* and its religious dimensions must attend to the movements by a variety of African Americans between the Black and white worlds.

ON THE MEANING OF BLACK SOUL STRUGGLES

As with any intellectual, DuBois's perspectives on religion and spirituality undoubtedly transformed throughout his lifetime. Nevertheless, he leaves in *Souls*, and the larger corpus of his work,[16] important source material for what I take to be a more expansive meaning of African American religious struggle *qua* the Black soul struggle, which is uniquely structured by US anti-blackness and white-hegemonic cultural practices that undergird and condition various kinds of psychic violence and limited life options that spur African-American religio-cultural action and expression.

Anti-blackness, as I utilize it here, refers to the systemic and pervasive prejudice, discrimination, and violence explicitly directed toward African American communities.[17] In the context of Black soul struggles, anti-blackness represents the oppressive forces and structures that seek to undermine the integrity of African American identity. Anti-blackness manifests in various forms, including institutional racism, racial stereotypes, microaggressions, and acts of violence. *The Black soul struggle, therefore, is the ongoing battle to build, maintain, and affirm one's sense of African-American identity in the face of these disintegrating forces. It involves the fight against the social, psychological (intellectual/mythical), and physical violence inflicted upon African Americans and their communities due to anti-blackness.*[18]

The Black soul struggle is both personal and collective. On a personal level, it involves the individual's quest for self-consciousness and self-acceptance in a society that perpetuates anti-blackness. It is about preserving one's dignity, self-worth, and cultural heritage in the face of dehumanization. On a collective level, the Black soul struggle encompasses the broader fight for the African-American community's recognition, empowerment, and liberation. It involves at least challenging—if one cannot dismantle—systems and structures that perpetuate anti-blackness. It also entails participating in work that seeks a more just and equitable society.

This essay emphasizes the ongoing battle for the Black soul as a constant struggle for significance and acceptance within the collective consciousness of Black (behind the Veil) and white (beyond the Veil) social arrangements. These two worlds constantly shape the daily experiences and perceptions of Black existence, exerting inexorable pressures on the lives of African Americans to "come to terms"[19] with who they are within the larger cognitive and cultural schemes that exists in their social worlds.

In *Souls*, Du Bois recounts a personal experience from childhood that serves as a starting point for understanding the Black soul's struggle for identity and belonging. He shares an incident where, as a young boy, he innocently offers a visiting schoolgirl a card with his name written on it as a gesture of friendship. However, the girl rejects the card and refuses to associate with him because of her racial consciousness, namely, that she is white and DuBois is Black. This encounter profoundly impacts Du Bois, as it becomes his first direct experience of personal disintegration. In this moment, he becomes aware of a divide between what he had previously believed to be a sense of belonging—a fellow student and companion in young development—and a newfound understanding of his Black existence.[20] This moment serves as the impulse for DuBois to come to terms with his racial identity. He embarks on a journey of self-discovery, determined to at least confront the violent psychic injustices inflicted upon himself and other African Americans.

Du Bois's narrative establishes a connection with broader struggles for self-definition and belonging faced by African Americans. He underscores the personal dimension of the Black soul struggle. In his case, he decides to out-perform any white "in-group" he had to encounter as a part of his "Black excellence" orientation and identity vis-à-vis the elite, Black "Talented Tenth."[21]

DuBois does go on to describe how this struggle is perceived by different groups of African Americans working in various sectors of society—e.g., the preacher, the artisan—illumining a range of Black racial struggles (and implications) in relationship to that horrible "gift" of second sightedness. Through their moral/spiritual leadership roles in the community, preachers, for instance, become acutely aware of the racial disparities and injustices African Americans face because they are often on the front lines as firsthand witnesses to the lives of their congregants. Black artisans and workers gain a heightened awareness of the racial barriers and limitations imposed upon them on the job as their talents and skills are regularly undervalued and marginalized. I should note that I term the gift of second-sightedness horrible—not DuBois—because I find it paradoxical that African American visions of life must always form against the backdrop of "looking at one's [Black] self through the revelation of the other [white] world."[22] DuBois is right about it being a gift, however. Because the uniquely American genius and resolve required—or rather formed—to have a healthy sense of Black consciousness and identity in American society is nothing short of remarkable.

What does all of this say about the meaning of Black soul struggles? As a recap, I take the Black soul struggle to mean African Americans' constant individual and shared struggle to arrive at a healthy sense of self-definition. It is a fundamental desire I think DuBois illumines—a desire to adequately self-determine one's sense of selfhood and community in a way that best suits one for courageous engagement within the US democratic experiment, and to do so with integrity and passion.

ON THE NATURE OF BLACK SOUL STRUGGLES AND THE IMPORTANCE OF HBCUs

Considering DuBois's thoughts about African American life and its development, attending to the *intra*-communal aspects of the Black soul struggle is vital. While DuBois's work highlights a duality and collective nature of American identity work, focusing on the white gaze, it doesn't consider the various intersectional struggles in African American community life.

Intersectionality as a perspective recognizes that individuals have multiple identities and experiences that intersect with their race—related to gender, sexuality, and social class, to name a few. Scholars and activists like Patricia Hill Collins and Kimberlé Crenshaw have emphasized the need for more robust intersectional analysis when it comes to discussions of Black racial oppression. They push analysts to consider how intersectional issues of gender and sex, especially, shape and complicate the experiences of African Americans within the broader struggle for meaning and recognition.[23] Acknowledging the intersectionality of identities helps one develop a more nuanced understanding of Black soul struggles. It recognizes the complexity and variations within the Black community, challenging the notion of a singular Black experience and highlighting the need for inclusive and comprehensive approaches to interpreting Black religious expression.

At least two points can be made here about the above complexities involved in Black soul struggles. For one, an embodiment approach would make explorations more robust as it relates to the nature of Black soul struggles. This means more focused attention on the African American body—how it moves, how we adorn it, and how we instruct it—will add valuable insights. Although the Black body is tacitly there in Du Bois's work, much more can be said about the kinds of strivings of what one might call the *blackest* of Black bodies. If Black existence in the US is something to be thought of as unenviable, then what about being Black and queer, Black and woman, Black and poor—all intersections that carry with them different kinds of experience and marginalization that refract back into the African American community competing moral visions for representation and forming young adults and future leaders.

Explorations in embodiment and its dual nature—specifically on the relationship between the Black soul struggle and the African-American cultural representations and orientations that emerge from such struggle—enhance one's comprehension of the intricacies of African-American identity formation. It is another way of uncovering the complexity of self-definition as African Americans are formed in a variety of social worlds, there is no one Black existence by which African Americans are formed.[24] An embodiment approach that seeks to interpret the larger social contexts in which individuals are formed acknowledges the complex interplay between personal agency and collective consciousness. While individuals can shape their orientations and pursue their interests and desires alone in a sense, they nonetheless do so as they move in and are influenced by broader social contexts in which they exist.

As I noted above, HBCUs have been some of the most important social institutions for African Americans in their struggle for identity. They are important *social bodies* that influence the personal agency and formation of students and future leaders. These institutions have served as spaces where

African Americans can develop their intellectual and cultural identities, often in response to the limitations and exclusion they faced historically in predominantly white institutions and spaces.

My discussion of HBCUs as a critical *social* body leads me to another point about embodiment studies and what it contributes to the analysis of Black soul struggles. Namely, that we all belong to two different kinds of "bodies," as it were. Important to understanding one's individual development is to understand that we belong to "social bodies." Social bodies are those environments or entities that configure scripts into which we are written (or born) and perform based on the external pressures within social arrangements. The controls or "powers" within these social arrangements—be they authorities, ideas, ritual practices, symbols, and various other representations—inform how we go on to define ourselves.[25] Following this train of thought—considering HBCUs in the vein of powerful Black social bodies—then we can better understand what the best approaches might be for a variety of HBCUs today. They remain as preeminent training grounds for young Black professional, intellectuals, and civic leaders preparing for tomorrow's ethical and cultural challenges. Moreover, given the new moral demands presented by our youth and their embrace of what one might call a new cultural politics of *difference,* we must critically assess, again, HBCU educational and mentoring formation models, tailoring them better to fit a growing communal acceptance of plural expressions of African American identity, meaning, and social belonging.

In summary, the study of embodiment vis-à-vis the Black soul struggle provides an essential lens through which we not only analyze and understand how African Americans navigate their identities and experiences within white worlds, but it also highlights the material realities and lived experiences of Black people contesting for a sense of belonging and identity within Black collectives. This is of crucial importance today, as a significant number of HBCUs play a vital role in providing education and assistance to Black students who are the first in their families to pursue higher education,[26] and face additional challenges that we must address in their training before we send them into white-dominant worlds that will seek to beat back their confidence. Considering the intricate psychological and social aspects involved in their development and the values they might hold dear; we must focus more consistently on addressing conflicts and tensions within the HBCU community regarding the most effective approaches and perspectives for educating and preparing undergraduate students in their Black soul struggles.

Secondly, of particular importance here, is that DuBois's metaphors serve prophetically to push analysts of African American culture to investigate more about the nature of the Black soul struggle as they are prominently shaped *behind/within* the Veil. It's one thing to note the "measuring tapes" of white supremacist onlookers who show contempt for Black life with evaluative standards deemed "objective" but de facto only serve to exacerbate inequality between Black and white existence. However, it is an entirely different matter when Black communities, in part due to necessary historical practices of assimilation to mainstream American life, fail to account seriously for its intra-community differences, differences that also significantly shape how we go about educating and training students and future leaders to compete in modern global society. Thus, by understanding how the material ways of being and experiencing within the Black community, particularly within the context of HBCUs in this case, one gains valuable insights into the nature of individual and group Black soul struggles that arise for the next generation of African-American leaders. There are a range of complex negotiations, exchanges, and interactions that shape the experiences of African Americans on campuses.

ON RELIGION AND THE "RELIGIOUS" IN BLACK SOUL STRUGGLES

At this juncture, it's necessary to account for some of the ways I conceive the Black Soul struggle to be religious. Here, I turn to the work of scholars Charles Long and Anthony Pinn (and, to a lesser extent, Orlando Patterson).[27] Historian of religion Charles Long helps in this task by broadening the parameters for how one might interpret the meaning of African-American religious struggle. Following Long and his explications of the work involved in how communities "come to terms" with themselves within commanding mythical-knowledge arrangements to create themselves anew, I first deem Black Soul struggles religious because of what I see as their psychic-intellectual struggle through a variety of sophisticated negative stereotypes and categorizations often hidden in "significations." Charles Long defines *signification* as the process by which signs create and communicate meaning. He argues that signs are not inherently meaningful but gain meaning through their association with other signs and their context within a particular cultural and social framework. Signification involves the interpretation and understanding of signs and the production and dissemination of signs to convey meaning. Long emphasizes the role of language, symbols, and gestures in signification but also acknowledges the importance of nonverbal and visual forms of communication. Overall, signification is a complex and dynamic process that shapes our understanding of the world and our interactions with others.[28]

For Long, one must interpret religious practice within the context and emergence of symbols, signs, and images amid worlds affected by power (e.g., colonial contact), cultural difference (Other-ing), and modernity (i.e., the struggle for the authority of ideas and interpretation of reality).[29] His corpus helps one to begin to understand a complexity of African-American religious meaning-making as a *mythical-intellectual* tussle with or against those who possess the arbitrary power of naming and reifying the status, meaning, and humanity of others. Religious signification, then, following Long (and Orlando Patterson), can be thought of as one way in which those in power establish authority by their naming power—by their ability to reify the status of others in authoritative symbolic clusters of meaning which work to maintain society and its system of controls.[30]

Concerning African-American life, there are undeniable and widespread realities that signify what I call, following theorist Orlando Patterson, Black "social death"[31]—e.g., hyper-unemployment and imprisonment, disparity in medical and healthcare. Black social death is itself a dominant cultural symbol[32] for the seemingly intentional cultural processes that permanently establish the alienation of African Americans as something "Other."[33] It refracts through different knowledge frameworks, modes of being, and cultural practices—be they military, corporate, or prison industrial complexes. Moreover, within *specific* American social-cultural arrangements (and the signs, symbols, and ritual practices available therein), African Americans struggle to counter the depictions, productions, and ritual practices that seek to overwhelm (or snuff out!) Black lives.

Authentically, African Americans have always managed to create life for themselves, carving out important social space for meaningful identity and belonging—e.g., within Black churches and HBCUs—in wider public life. Yet, one still sees that African Americans must utilize whatever discursive and material means available to them to create *newer* self-definitions and significance which counter negative narratives and perceptions of Black humanity in other contexts that matter to them. Long's work then authenticates a complex array of creative intellectual/mythical genius and work that is part and parcel of the African-American religious struggle. Applying Long to a socio-historical understanding of religious struggle, I consider African-American religious struggle an incomplete, never-ending, tussle in history for a sense of meaningful identity and social belonging (or life)— a resilient wishing to *signify* that those African American lives matter.

Long's definition of religion is rather unconventional (as is the case for most religious studies scholars seeking to offer some general understanding of the nature and meaning of religious practice).[34] After surveying the history of religious formations across the world, Long comes to understand religious struggle to entail attempts at world-orientation—what he refers to as a kind of "orientation in the ultimate sense." Here, what is at work is an attempt to "come to terms with the ultimate significance of one's place in the world."[35] Such a definitional range permits Long to find Black religious expressions in a variety of Black cultural traditions, such as in folklore, music, or other "styles of life," as he puts it.[36] And, as I'll show, it is precisely along the lines other styles of life and the formation of worldly-orientations that the work of HBCUs take center stage.

Long helps illumine Black Soul struggle as a religious struggle, a mythic/intellectual exertion, by elucidating how dominant culture (or power) signifies authority in and through a variety of meaning-making arrangements, which requires one to disentangle the sinister and sincere significations within such arrangement to discover one's authentic sense of self.[37] Thus, in reading Long, one notices that it becomes hard to interpret religious struggle outside of how it takes place in the context of modernity—itself a complex figuration of power (colonial) and perceived group (European) superiority that works under the guise of rationalization to legitimate the (hierarchical) order of things. Long, thus, pushes scholars to reveal the hidden meanings of power in symbolic content. Nevertheless, the best route to discover these meanings is from the perspective of those who have historically been on the underside of power, namely, those who struggle for forms of "independent consciousness" (or autonomy) in identity that minimizes "the economic, political, and linguistic hegemony" of dominant culture.[38] Hence, Black Soul struggles are religious, following Long, in that they all attempt to wrestle with sophisticated ideas and representations—symbols and signs and images—to establish meaningful identity anew in worlds often created by powerful others who signify African-American inferiority.

Another significant theorist for understanding the Black soul struggle *qua* religious struggle, and who builds on Long's work, is Anthony Pinn.[39] However, most importantly, perhaps no other theorist of African-American religion has commented more substantively on the centrality of the *body* and the material nature of African-American religious meaning-making. Following Pinn, one could also state that at the core of African-American religious struggle is the desire to escape such trappings, to *physically* (re) locate one's Black body in healthier environments that permit more comprehensive ranges (e.g., symbols, languages, practices) for expressing that Black life matters.[40]

For Pinn, African-American religious reality is a processual "quest for complex subjectivity," as he terms it, or a continual yearning and meaning-making activity (cultural production) by Blacks for a liberated self which manifests itself in history through various modalities that yet contain a more profound yearning for *more*.[41] The significance for Pinn's early theorizing of Black struggle becomes apparent under the light of African-American history; or rather the more extended cultural narrative of how Black bodies have been shaped as objects in (and for) this country.[42] Thus the movement from historical object to modern subject is essential to the African-American religious quest for Pinn. Hence, being African American *and* religious means constantly engaging in projects that resist whatever efforts are at work to beat Black bodies into reified (historical) objects. Pinn documents some of the most egregious cultural practices of objectification and social control against Black bodies in

American history (i.e., slave auction blocks and lynching during times of segregation) as "rituals of reference"— again, symbolic social practices that kept Black bodies in place and maintained their status as discardable, inferior, and in need of management.[43] As I suggest above, the ritual practice of signaling Black bodies unworthy of life and need of constant control and management via physical means is still rampant in US social life. As such, an essential aspect of any analysis of the Black Soul struggle requires explicit attention to what constitutes the African-American body and how it shapes religious meaning-making.

Again, this brings to the fore how HBCUs are important social bodies that shape and develop how a variety of young African Americans come to understand their individuality and personhood. Pinn frames the nature of the body and its symbolic significance by building upon the work of influential social theorists Mary Douglas,[44] Michael Foucault,[45] and by applying other critical perspectives from sociology of the body.[46] Utilizing these perspectives, Pinn constructs an inseparable compound body, which is particularly visible vis-à-vis Black bodies.

A simplification of Pinn's compound body is this: "Every-body" is not only "biochemical" stuff, the flesh, sinews, and bones that we constitute and can touch, but he/she/they is also a socially constructed, "discursive" reality.[47] The latter, socially constructed body is an extension of the physical body, constituted by inherited ideas and knowledge structures; cultural arrangements and ideations (e.g., through media); and social practices which embed the ways (e.g., religious, academic, community-related, etc.) one comes to know and interpret humanity and cultural difference. Therefore, as different Black composite bodies appear in time and space—as they appear materially in social contexts like HBCUs and in broader publics— they are "being read" in multiple ways. Past and present understandings of Black bodies—along the lines of race, class, sex, and so on— inform certain biases concerning how they are received and rendered. Attention to this dynamism through embodiment (body) analysis, or what Melling and Shilling call "body pedagogics,"[48] helps one better understand some of the differentiated concerns of various African-American social groups and yields more comprehension concerning complexity and contingency which shape the meaning of Black soul (religious) struggle in contemporary US.

The theorists I adduce above and the intellectual traditions they represent all stress different but important qualities about the nature of the Black Soul struggle *as* a religious struggle. In short, they confirm that the Black soul struggle is religious in that it is an ongoing historical attempt to bring about African-American life in contestation with the myriad symbolic and ritual realities that suggest what is tantamount to Black social death in America today.

WITHIN (OR BEHIND) THE VEIL: ON THE SOUL STRUGGLES OF HBCUs

To claim that HBCUs are necessary institutional arrangements and resources in the *religious* mission of the Black soul struggle should not appear too untenable. First, on an explicit level, most HBCUs were founded with some sense of religious mission. Historian Bobby Lovett notes that most of the nineteenth-century curricula of HBCUs "reflected the religious and educational philosophy of Northern missionaries"[49] who, along with white abolitionists and philanthropists, were responsible for many of their formations. Religion and moral living, liberal arts, civic education, and loyalty to America were recurrent themes of HBCU curricula. In fact, early on, HBCUs focused on the training of ministers, industrial workers, artisans, and teachers.[50] These emphases are still operative at many HBCUs today and embedded within some HBCU mission statements are the moral and spiritual development of their students.[51]

Beyond the pale of traditional religious affiliation and mission, however, HBCUs are critical for shaping healthy psychic and narrative (intellectual/ mythical) histories for students from various backgrounds. Students need guides as they interrogate the African American experience as a complex tapestry of struggle, resilience, and triumph. To some extent, students will come to HBCU campuses with a family history of a rare spiritual resilience they will need to disentangle in coming to terms with "who they are" against the larger backdrop of anti-blackness, alienation, and despair in a white-dominated society. At HBCUs, they should encounter safe Black social environments that regard them "within the Veil" in educational and developmental communities that nurture healthy senses of African-American self-definition and determination early on.

HBCUs play a crucial role here, even as they themselves are subject to some of the same rampant issues of structural inequality and neglect that Black communities face—particularly as it relates to historic underfunding. Nonetheless, HBCUs have proven to enhance the social mobility of students who attend and have especially contributed to the advancement and livelihood of Black and low-income families. Their accessibility and affordability make them vital pillars of hope for the educational development in many of our African-American urban and rural communities.[52] It is essential, then, that young undergraduates who enter the doors of HBCUs during such pivotal stages in their personal and intellectual development are met with a kind of institutional intention and care they deserve. Such intention and care, to be sure, will involve affirmation for their developing sense of Black selves. However, it also involves installations of ripe confidence, revealing to students how they possess the moral and intellectual capacity to become significant change agents in life and thought—in keeping with the great lore and ancestral legacies about which their HBCUs boast.

Just how each HBCU accomplishes this will differ. Each HBCU, with its unique history and cultural context, has the potential to shape its curriculum and campus culture in a way that reflects the distinct needs and aspirations of its student population. This, of course, means incorporating elements of African American history and culture into all curricula subjects. But it also means fostering a sense of community and *accountability* by providing needed mentorship and support services that address the specific challenges faced by students of color in various fields of endeavor.

Moreover, by leveraging historical consciousness, HBCUs can inspire students to strive for excellence and to make positive impacts on their communities. By highlighting the achievements of past alumni and the struggles they overcame, these institutions can instill a sense of pride and resilience in their students which will be needed as they continue to define themselves in vocation and community. Equally important, HBCUs must continue to play a crucial role in promoting social justice and equality. Through their research, community outreach, and advocacy efforts, they must instill important lessons social and community responsibility in the ongoing fight against racial discrimination and social inequality. None of these efforts are new. HBCUs have always been known for their long-standing commitments to community outreach, public service, and racial uplift.[53] But a renewed and adapted focused is needed, given the changing of times. While the methods may vary, the overall mission of HBCUs as it relates to the Black soul struggle remains the same: to provide a high-quality education that empowers students of color and prepares them for success in a diverse and global society. This mission, coupled with their historical consciousness positions HBCUs to create a unique and transformative educational experience that will no doubt help students shape the kind of critical Black consciousness needed for tomorrow's world.

FUTURE DIRECTIONS IN HBCU PARTICIPATION CONTEMPORARY BLACK SOUL STRUGGLE

Today, HBCUs stand at the precipice of a new era, poised to produce a new generation of leaders and intellectuals who are not only aware of the struggles of marginalized African Americans but are also equipped to address them. The 2020s marked yet another palpable shift in the critical and cultural consciousness of Black America. Amid a global pandemic, we also witnessed the largest global racial justice movement in history. Public discourse about the murders of George Floyd and Breonna Taylor loomed large, and corporations and federal government agencies alike began to look for ways to tangibly support Black communities. With such broad exposure, we began to hear anew, from Black Gen-Z activists and students, the previous decade's complaints by Black Millennials against the stubborn respectability traditions often proffered by Black institutions.

In Richmond (VA), young students, and activists at Virginia Union University (VUU) saw the toppling of Confederate statues along a symbolically important route and street in the city called Monument Avenue. Against this backdrop, I began working as a professor, administrator, and leader among gifted undergraduates aged 18–25. And in the last three years, I have become acquainted with an impressive VUU's history, lore, and mission within the larger HBCU domain. I have also come to discover that those of us who feel summoned by HBCU assignments can and must participate positively in our students' and institutions' long struggle for and on behalf of the African American soul by ensuring that our educational delivery meets the specific needs of our student-constituent communities.

One important HBCU delivery strategy that will aide students in their quest for self-understanding and meaning involves developing intergenerational acuity. Intergenerational acuity is a strategy that involves fostering meaningful connections and interactions between different generations within the HBCU community. This approach recognizes the value of wisdom, experience, and knowledge that senior faculty and administrators can offer to younger generations, while also acknowledging the fresh perspectives and innovative ideas that younger generations bring. By creating opportunities for mentorship, dialog, collaboration, and involvement in educational processes, HBCUs can harness the collective wisdom and experiences of older generations while empowering younger generations to contribute their fresh perspectives and ideas. This approach enriches the educational and developmental training at HBCUs, creating a vibrant and inclusive community.

At HBCUs, intergenerational acuity can be implemented through various initiatives and activities. For example, mentorship programs can pair older students or alumni with younger students, allowing for guidance, support, and the sharing of experiences. This mentorship can extend beyond academic matters and encompass personal and professional development as well. Intergenerational acuity can also be fostered through intergenerational dialog and collaboration. HBCUs can organize events, workshops, or panel discussions that bring together students, faculty, staff, and alumni from different generations. These platforms provide opportunities for individuals to share their insights, perspectives, and experiences, creating a rich learning environment where knowledge is exchanged and relationships are built.

Furthermore, HBCUs can leverage the expertise and experience of faculty and senior administrators by involving them in curriculum development, guest lectures, or advisory roles. This allows for the integration of real-world knowledge and practical insights into the educational experience of younger students. By promoting intergenerational acuity, HBCUs can create a supportive and inclusive environment where students can benefit from the wisdom and guidance, while also being encouraged to bring their unique perspectives and ideas to the table. This strategy not only enhances the educational experience but also helps students develop a sense of belonging, respect, and appreciation for the diverse voices within the African American community. Some professors at HBCUs take such work seriously. Stories abound about how HBCU professors have historically been invested highly in students' success and development; and, unlike at many predominantly white institutionss, some professor-student relationships take on a somewhat "pastoral" dimension. I must note that, although such cultural-kinship ties are not uncommon, they can be and have been misused. Yet, employed correctly they can enable one of the most transformative experiences in a student's educational development.

Another strategy for aiding HBCU students is to design and implement innovative pedagogical strategies that combine forms of intellectual rigor with custom forms of care for the Black psyches of our students. Furthermore, after some years of listening to the students, I have found that, more than anything, they need safe spaces for learning. Here, I am referring to intellectual safety. Nevertheless, one cannot divorce intellectual safety from the psychic and emotional safety needed for intellectual growth, which has been absent from many of our students' lives. Two parts to this are essential. For one, I have found resonance with many of the thinkers and the ideas presented in the courses and public discussions; and so, for many of our students, the content we teach in the humanities is already embedded in their intellectual DNA. For example, if I teach about Black religion, hip-hop culture, or ethics and politics in Black Communities, the concerns and issues raised are not new to them. I merely provide language for them, a new lexicon for public discourse and self-understanding that helps them in their self-realization struggle.

Mindful of the above, it is important to incorporate diverse perspectives into curricula. Sometimes, this is a challenge, given general core education foci. However, there are ways to include various voices and perspectives—particularly those historically marginalized by the broader discourses we teach. Exposing students to diverse perspectives will expand their understanding of the world and provide them with a broader vocabulary for engaging in public discourse. They do not have to agree with the various perspectives presented, but this also leads to another critical point. We must encourage critical thinking and analysis while providing safe platforms for expressions from our students. On a personal note, in addition to creative ways to discuss and exchange ideas in class, I have often had students and interns participate with me in and prepare for events that allow them to share their perspectives and engage in meaningful dialog with their peers and the wider community. By providing platforms for expression, HBCUs empower students to contribute to public discourse and shape the narrative around issues that matter to them the most. This pushes students to hone their ideas while fostering cultures of respect and open-mindedness among them. By implementing these strategies, HBCUs can provide students with a new lexicon for public discourse and self-understanding. This approach empowers students to articulate their thoughts and ideas effectively, engage in meaningful dialog, and contribute to shaping public narratives. Ultimately, it helps students in their self-realization struggle by providing them with the tools and language to navigate the world's complexities and express their unique *perspectives.*

However, as we scrutinize how HBCUs function as social bodies for future Black leaders' educational and identity formation, we must also attend to student developmental concerns and the range of experiences and expressions they bring to HBCU campuses. For example, the challenges faced by first-generation LGBTQI+ students at HBCUs and young Black male students navigating different modes of masculinist expression highlight the need for a nuanced understanding of the struggles faced by individuals within the Black community. Furthermore, we *must* attend more to issues of African-American social class. It impacts the resources, opportunities, and thus, even the veritable "success" how one dogged Black soul might even dare struggle.

Next, we can aid students in their soul struggles by *helping them tap into the unique cultural histories of their HBCU institutions in ways that inspire them toward their uniqueness.* Here I contend that every HBCU has a thread, or threads, of connection that can be used to inspire student toward realizing their potential. It is a simple statement that remains true: if you exhibit intellectual care that comes through the precision of what we present to them, then we can see explosions in intellectual creativity and vocational awareness among our students. Virginia Union, for instance, has a powerful historical narrative around women founders and pioneers of education civic leadership. Founded in 1865 after a parcel of land was dedicated by a formerly enslaved woman, Mary Lumpkin, it is our responsibility to excavate VUU's stories like hers, not only for broader academic, critical intellectual engagement, but also as motivation and inspiration for young people who are a part of her legacy.

Finally, I contend that HBCUs engage in what might be termed a spiritual pedagogy, whereby we teach our students to "read the signs." Ultimately, we must teach them to subvert the system, not to be ashamed of what shapes their intellectual interests and desires and develop their critical capacities in ways that release their genius. To do this, however, we—those of us training/teaching—must be willing to learn in a dialectical, creative exchange with our learners. In other words, as we introduce and foster new knowledge capacities and vocational competencies in our students, in keeping with the best academic paradigms, we must also encourage them to identify and interpret the wiles at play in the worlds we're preparing them to enter.

In many ways, we are teaching students to esteem rationalization and scientific inquiry and training as keys to their future "success." In truth, however, we are training them to enter new language and practice communities because the education and training provided to our students, particularly in academic settings, goes beyond simply imparting knowledge and skills. Instead, it prepares them to become part of specific communities that have their own unique language, practices, and ways of operating. I teach my HBCU students that when engaged in higher education or specialized training, they are exposed to new disciplines, fields of study, and professional environments. Each of these domains has its own set of terminology, concepts, methodologies, and ways of thinking. By immersing themselves in these academic or professional communities, they are not only acquiring knowledge but also learning how to communicate effectively within these specific contexts.

Many of these new language communities will devalue and demean their Black formative existence in ways they'll have to combat. And, they will need to do so by pulling from lessons learned in carefully augmented instruction by those faculty and mentors attuned to the broader white-world logics and significations in all their forms. This might be the last work we do before sending them to new clever worlds "beyond the Veil." As they become comfortable in these new worlds, they'll remember the subtle tricks of those on the other side and challenge the sign games against them, and in this way not "loose themselves." My students often hear it from those within the Veil—"skin folks who ain't kinfolk"—who ask: "Hey," they say, "you do realize VUU is a second-chance school, not a school of choice in VA?" When I hear this question, I suggest to my students that the ignorance which undergirds these assaults by those who should know better is more deleterious to the assailants. I advise that they hardly think about responding to such barbs, but instead, they reply in the same way I hear them signify among each other: "Be fuckin' for real."

HBCUs hold a matchless power in the world today. They have a long-standing history of providing higher education opportunities to African American students, particularly during times of racial segregation and limited access to mainstream institutions. These institutions have played a crucial role in fostering academic excellence, promoting cultural awareness, and nurturing leadership skills among Black students. Furthermore, HBCUs have often been at the forefront of social and political movements, advocating for civil rights, equality, and social justice. They have produced influential leaders, intellectuals, and activists who have made significant contributions to various fields, including politics, arts, sciences, and business.

African Americans from various contexts come for educational formation, personal development, and self-realization before struggling forward with generations of Black folks cheering them on. I'm convinced that all

HBCUs have this rich narrative knowledge and devoted students, faculty, staff, and alumni that mark them as great boons for shaping the future of Black America.

NOTES

1. W. E. B. DuBois, *The Souls of Black Folk*, Reissue edition, ed. Brent Hayes Edwards (Oxford: Oxford University Press, 2009).
2. Charles Long, *Significations: Signs, Symbols, and Images in the Interpretation of Religion*, 2nd ed. (Aurora, CO: The Davies Group Publishers, 1986).
3. My first engagement with the subject of religious struggle in higher education contexts was some time ago in relation Black Greek Letter Organization formations and it remains compelling to me. See CERCL Writing Collective, "School Daze: Embodiment and Meaning-Making in Black-Greek Letter Organizations," in *Embodiment and Black Religion: Rethinking the Body in African American Religious Experience* (Bristol, CT: Equinox, 2017): 82–93.
4. Bobby L. Lovett, *America's Historically Black Colleges and Universities: A Narrative History, 1837-2009*, Reprint edition (Macon, GA: Mercer University Press, 2015).
5. I'm referring here to the ways of greeting, to the pronouncements of alma maters, to the everyday rituals of HBCUs that evoke deep kinship ties.
6. Theophus H. Smith, *Conjuring Culture: Biblical Formations of Black America* (New York: Oxford University Press, 1995); Yvonne P. Chireau, *Black Magic: Religion and the African American Conjuring Tradition*, 1st ed. (Berkeley: University of California Press, 2006); Peter J. Paris, *The Social Teaching of the Black Churches* (Philadelphia, PA: Augsburg Fortress Publishers, 1998); Peter J. Paris, ed., *The Spirituality of African Peoples: The Search for a Common Moral Discourse* (Minneapolis, MN: Fortress Press, 1994).
7. Travis Mitchell, "Faith Among Black Americans." *Pew Research Center's Religion & Public Life Project* (blog), February 16, 2021. https://www.pewresearch.org/religion/2021/02/16/faith-among-black-americans/
8. Paris, *The Social Teaching of the Black Churches*, 116; Lovett, *America's Historically Black Colleges and Universities*, 140–86.
9. Eddie S. Glaude Jr., "The Black Church Is Dead | HuffPost Religion," accessed September 26, 2023 https://www.huffpost.com/entry/the-black-church-is-dead_b_473815; Rahiel Tesfamariam, "Why the Modern Civil Rights Movement Keeps Religious Leaders at Arm's Length." *Washington Post*, September 18, 2015. https://www.washingtonpost.com/opinions/how-black-activism-lost-its-religion/2015/09/18/2f56fc00-5d6b-11e5-8e9e-dce8a2a2a679_story.html
10. Melvin Oliver, and Thomas M. Shapiro, eds., *Black Wealth/White Wealth: A New Perspective on Racial Inequality*, 2nd ed. (New York: Routledge, 2006); For a great sociological overview about the disparities shaped by Black racial formations in the US, see Michael Omi and Howard Winant, *Racial Formation in the United States*, 3rd ed. (New York: Routledge, 2014).

11. W. E. B. Du Bois, *The Souls of Black Folk*.

12. W. E. B. Du Bois, *The Souls of Black Folk*, ed. David W. Blight and Robert Gooding-Williams, 1st ed. (Boston, MA: Bedford/St. Martin's, 1997): 2–7.

13. Anthony B. Pinn, "DuBois' Souls: Thoughts on 'Veiled' Bodies and the Study of Black Religion." *The North Star: A Journal of African American Religious History*, 6, no. 2 (Spring, 2003): 1–5. https://www.princeton.edu/~jweisenf/northstar/volume6/pinn.html; Terrence L. Johnson, *Tragic Soul-Life: W.E.B. Du Bois and the Moral Crisis Facing American Democracy*, 1st ed. (New York: Oxford University Press, 2012); Henry Louis Gates Jr and Cornel West, *The Future of the Race*, Reprint edition. (New York: Vintage, 1997).

14. Du Bois, *The Souls of Black Folk*, 2009, 128–40.

15. Ibid., 226.

16. Du Bois, *The Souls of Black Folk*, 1997; W. E. B. Du Bois, *Darkwater: Voices from Within the Veil* (Mineola, NY: Dover Publications, 1999); W. E. B. Du Bois, *The Gift of Black Folk: The Negroes in the Making of America*, ed. Carl A. Anderson and Edward Francis McSweeney (New York: Square One Pub., 2009); W. E. B. Du Bois, and D. L. Lewis, *Black Reconstruction in America (The Oxford W. E. B. Du Bois): An Essay Toward a History of the Part Which Black Folk Played in the Attempt to Reconstruct Democracy in America, 1860-1880*, Ed. Henry Louis Gates, 1st ed. (Oxford: Oxford University Press, 2014).

17. For a recent and compelling study on Anti-blackness as a phenomenon, see Moon-Kie Jung and João H. Costa Vargas, eds., *Antiblackness* (Durham, NC: Duke University Press Books, 2021).

18. I also will later term the psychological struggle in terms of mythical-intellectual struggle. It's an attempt to "wrap ones' mind around" what it means to exist authentically in specific social and knowledge arrangements without "losing" oneself or sense of self.

19. I use "come to terms" here and elsewhere thinking about the kinds of cognitive and psychic struggle within which African Americans are always embroiled within different contexts and community languages of meaning.

20. Du Bois, *The Souls of Black Folk*, 1997, 2–7.

21. Du Bois, *The Souls of Black Folk*, 2009, 226.

22. Du Bois, *The Souls of Black Folk*, 1997, 9.

23. Kimberlé Crenshaw, *On Intersectionality: Essential Writings* (New York: The New Press, 2019); Patricia Hill Collins, *Black Feminist Thought: Knowledge, Consciousness, and the Politics of Empowerment* (Boston, MA: Uwin Hyman, 1990).

24. Many African Americans, for example, are formed in biracial worlds or in predominately white environments which affect how they go on to construct their self-definition. See, as an example.

25. For important cultural theory on the body and embodiment and more detailed discussion on the relationship between the social body and the individual see Mary Douglas, *Natural Symbols: Explorations in Cosmology*, Vintage Books edition. (New York: Pantheon Books, 1973); Mike Hepworth, Bryan S. Turner, and Mike Featherstone, eds., *The Body: Social Process and Cultural Theory* (London; Newbury Park, CA: SAGE Publications Ltd, 1991).

26. "About HBCUs." *Thurgood Marshall College Fund* (blog). https://www.tmcf.org/about-us/member-schools/about-hbcus/ accessed September 30, 2023.

27. Charles H. Long, "Assessment and New Departures for a Study of Black Religion in the United States," in *African American Religious Thought: An Anthology*, ed. Cornel West and Eddie S Glaude Jr. (Louisville, KY: Westminster John Knox Press, 2003): 221–38; Long, *Significations: Signs, Symbols, and Images in the Interpretation of Religion*; Charles H. Long, ed., *The Collected Writings of Charles H. Long: Ellipsis* (New York: Bloomsbury Academic, 2018); Orlando Patterson, *Slavery and Social Death: A Comparative Study*, 1st ed. (Cambridge, MA: Harvard University Press, 1982); Anthony B. Pinn, *Embodiment and the New Shape of Black Theological Thought* (New York: NYU Press, 2010).

28. See Long, *Significations*, especially 61–71.

29. Long, *Significations*; Long, *The Collected Writings of Charles H. Long.*

30. Here I combine Long's sophisticated analysis of religious meanings in the signs and significations of the "oppressed" groups by dominant groups with the stirring work of Orlando Patterson who in "Slavery and Social Death" argues that the subjection of slaves to the authority of "masters" who were often outnumbered related to the latter groups ability to establish symbolic control.

31. Orlando Patterson, "Authority, Alienation, and Social Death," in *African American Religious Thought: An Anthology*, ed. Cornel West and Eddie S Glaude Jr. (Louisville, KY: Westminster John Knox Press, 2003): 99–155. Orlando Patterson employs the notion of social death to encapsulate the kinds of complex social-structural processes by which "masters" in premodern/modern slave societies symbolized their ideas of control over oppressed slave populations. Social death was the intentional processes permanently establishing the alienation of a slave in a new master-environ. After analyzing and comparing over 66 slave-holding societies around the globe, Patterson discovers that a prominent strategy used among masters to secure their power over slaves was to concentrate on constructing the natal alienation of a slave through different images of social death. Masters not only created ritual practices in community to negate a slave's social existence, but they also permanently marked their slaves' social death with understandings and representations of a slave's genetic inferiority. Hence, a slave's social death meant that she was scorned and precluded from meaningful social integration on the margins of master-environments, as well as *justifiably* subjected to draconian physical cruelty due to their less-than-human status. The most successful slave societies, in short, linked the existential inferiority and exclusion (social death) of a slave to that slave's ontological defectiveness.

32. Dominant symbols control ideas or key ritual expressions which make possible "the internal interpretation of symbolic processes on both the intellectual and social level." See Patterson, "Authority, Alienation, and Social Death," 99–103.

33. Through the means of dominant symbols—e.g., infidel, slave, Gentile, Jew, nigger, etc.—powerful social groups establish identity boundaries and exert pressures of assimilation onto others through the dominant symbol's ability to unify while transforming what may be disparate negative significations and social practices against an oppressed social group. African Americans share a core desire to eliminate the sting of Black social death, a "dominant" cultural symbol in American life which hovers over every aspect of African-American existence and hope for better life chances. See Victor W. Turner, Roger D.

Abrahams, and Alfred Harris, *The Ritual Process: Structure and Anti-structure*, 1st ed. (New York: Aldine Transaction, 1995): 28.

34. Jonathan Z. Smith, "Religion, Religions, Religious," in *Critical Terms for Religious Studies*, ed. M. C. Taylor (Chicago: The University of Chicago Press, 1998). Smith notes that all attempts to arrive at some general understanding and interpretation of religious phenomena is at best "second-order" attempts of scholarly investigation to describe the first-hand experiences of those we observe.

35. Long, *Significations*, 9–11.

36. Ibid.

37. Long, *Significations*; Long, "Assessment and New Departures for a Study of Black Religion in the United States," 221–38.

38. Long, "Assessment and New Departures for a Study of Black Religion in the United States," 221–38.

39. I glean from a range of his thought in texts and smaller pieces, such as Anthony B. Pinn, *Terror and Triumph* (Minneapolis, MN: Augsburg Fortress Publishers, 2003); Pinn, "DuBois' Souls: Thoughts on 'Veiled' Bodies and the Study of Black Religion"; Pinn, *Embodiment and the New Shape of Black Theological Thought*; Anthony B. Pinn, *The End of God-Talk: An African American Humanist Theology* (Oxford; New York: Oxford University Press, 2012).

40. Or as Pinn puts it, "to be a complex conveyer of cultural meaning." See Pinn, *Terror and Triumph*, 173.

41. Pinn, *Terror and Triumph*, 157–77.

42. Ibid., 158.

43. Pinn, *Terror and Triumph*.

44. Douglas, *Natural Symbols*.

45. Michel Foucault, *Power/Knowledge: Selected Interviews and Other Writings, 1972-1977*, 1st American Ed edition, Ed. Colin Gordon (New York: Vintage, 1980); Michel Foucault, *The Archaeology of Knowledge: And the Discourse on Language*, 3988th ed. (New York: Vintage, 1982); Michel Foucault, *The History of Sexuality, Vol. 3: The Care of the Self*, trans. Robert Hurley, Reprint edition (New York: Vintage, 1988); M. Foucault, *The History of Sexuality, Vol. 2: The Use of Pleasure*, trans. Robert Hurley , Reissue edition (New York: Vintage Books, 1990); Michel Foucault, *Discipline & Punish: The Birth of the Prison*, trans. Alan Sheridan (New York: Vintage Books, 1995).

46. Hepworth, Turner, and Featherstone, *The Body*; Philip A. Mellor and Chris Shilling, "Body Pedagogics and the Religious Habitus: A New Direction for the Sociological Study of Religion." *Religion*, 40, no. 1 (January 1, 2010): 27–38, https://doi.org/10.1016/j.religion.2009.07.001; Bryan S. Turner, *The Body and Society*, 3rd ed. (Los Angeles, CA: SAGE Publications Ltd, 2008).

47. Pinn, *Embodiment and the New Shape of Black Theological Thought*, 4–16.

48. Mellor and Shilling, "Body Pedagogics and the Religious Habitus."

49. Lovett, *America's Historically Black Colleges and Universities*, 22.

50. Ibid., 22–42.

51. A brief perusal of some prominent HBCUs in states along the African-American South confirms this. See, for instance, the missions of schools like Shaw University (https://www.shawu.edu/mission/?section=about-shaw#:~:text=Shaw%20University%20exists%20to%20advance,learners%20into%20future%20global%20leaders) and Virginia Union University (https://www.vuu.edu/vuusacs/vuusacs-mission).

52. Lian Herder, "UNCF Release Report Highlighting the Success of HBCUs at Moving Students Toward the Middle Class". *Diverse: Issues in Higher Education*, November 18, 2021. https://www.diverseeducation.com/institutions/hbcus/article/15281654/uncf-release-report-highlighting-the-success-of-hbcus-at-moving-students-toward-the-middle-class; Nathaniel Cline and Virginia Mercury, "Enrollment Is Growing at Virginia HBCUs. But They Face Historic Underfunding". *Virginia Mercury* (blog), October 3, 2023, https://www.virginiamercury.com/2023/10/03/enrollment-is-growing-at-virginia-hbcus-but-they-face-historic-underfunding/

53. Lovett, *America's Historically Black Colleges and Universities*, 138–85, 314–18.

REFERENCES

CERCL Writing Collective. "School Daze: Embodiment and Meaning-Making in Black-Greek Letter Organizations." In *Embodiment and Black Religion: Rethinking the Body in African American Religious Experience*, 82–93. Bristol, CT: Equinox, 2017.

Chireau, Yvonne Patricia. *Black Magic: Religion and the African American Conjuring Tradition*. 1st ed. Berkeley, CA: University of California Press, 2006.

Cline, Nathaniel, and Virginia Mercury. "Enrollment Is Growing at Virginia HBCUs. But They Face Historic Underfunding." *Virginia Mercury* (blog), October 3, 2023. https://www.virginiamercury.com/2023/10/03/enrollment-is-growing-at-virginia-hbcus-but-they-face-historic-underfunding/

Collins, Patricia Hill. *Black Feminist Thought: Knowledge, Consciousness, and the Politics of Empowerment*. Boston, MA: Uwin Hyman, 1990.

Crenshaw, Kimberlé. *On Intersectionality: Essential Writings*. New York, NY: The New Press, 2019.

Douglas, Mary. *Natural Symbols: Explorations in Cosmology*. Vintage Books edition. New York: Pantheon Books, 1973.

Du Bois, W. E. B. *Darkwater: Voices From Within the Veil*. Mineola, NY: Dover Publications, 1999.

Du Bois, W. E. B. *The Gift of Black Folk: The Negroes in the Making of America*. Edited by Carl A. Anderson and Edward Francis McSweeney. New York: Square One Pub., 2009.

Du Bois, W. E. B. *The Souls of Black Folk*. 1st ed. Edited by David W. Blight and Robert Gooding-Williams. Boston, MA: Bedford/St Martin's, 1997.

Du Bois, W. E. B. *The Souls of Black Folk*. Reissue edition. Edited by Brent Hayes Edwards. Oxford: Oxford University Press, 2009.

Du Bois, W. E. B., and Lewis, David Levering. *Black Reconstruction in America (The Oxford W. E. B. Du Bois): An Essay Toward a History of the Part Which Black Folk Played in the Attempt to Reconstruct Democracy in America, 1860-1880*. 1st ed. Edited by Henry Louis Gates. Oxford: Oxford University Press, 2014.

Foucault, Michel. *Discipline & Punish: The Birth of the Prison*. Translated by A. Sheridan. New York: Vintage Books, 1995.

Foucault, Michel. *Power/Knowledge: Selected Interviews and Other Writings, 1972-1977*. Edited by C. Gordon. 1st American Ed edition. New York: Vintage, 1980.

Foucault, Michel. *The Archaeology of Knowledge: And the Discourse on Language*. 3988th ed. New York: Vintage Books, 1982.

Foucault, Michel. *The History of Sexuality, Vol. 2: The Use of Pleasure*. Translated by R. Hurley. Reissue edition. New York: Vintage Books, 1990.

Foucault, Michel. *The History of Sexuality, Vol. 3: The Care of the Self*. Translated by R. Hurley. Reprint edition. New York: Vintage Books, 1988.

Glaude, Eddie S. Jr. "The Black Church Is Dead." *HuffPost Religion*. accessed September 26, 2023. https://www.huffpost.com/entry/the-black-church-is-dead_b_473815

Mike Hepworth, Bryan S. Turner, and Mike Featherstone, eds. *The Body: Social Process and Cultural Theory*. London; Newbury Park, CA: SAGE Publications Ltd, 1991.

Herder, Lian. "UNCF Release Report Highlighting the Success of HBCUs at Moving Students Toward the Middle Class." *Diverse: Issues In Higher Education*, November 18, 2021. https://www.diverseeducation.com/institutions/hbcus/article/15281654/uncf-release-report-highlighting-the-success-of-hbcus-at-moving-students-toward-the-middle-class

Johnson, Terrence L. *Tragic Soul-Life: W.E.B. Du Bois and the Moral Crisis Facing American Democracy*. 1st ed. New York: Oxford University Press, 2012.

Gates, Henry Louis Jr., and West, Cornel. *The Future of the Race*. Reprint edition. New York: Vintage, 1997.

Moon-Kie Jung and João H. Costa Vargas, eds., *Antiblackness*. Durham, NC: Duke University Press Books, 2021.

Long, Charles H. "Assessment and New Departures for a Study of Black Religion in the United States." In *African American Religious Thought: An Anthology*, edited by Cornel West and Eddie S. Glaude Jr., 221–38. Louisville, KY: Westminster John Knox Press, 2003.

Long, Charles H. *Significations: Signs, Symbols, and Images in the Interpretation of Religion*. 2nd ed. Aurora, CO: The Davies Group Publishers, 1986.

Charles H. Long, ed. *The Collected Writings of Charles H. Long: Ellipsis*. New York: Bloomsbury Academic, 2018.

Lovett, Bobby L. *America's Historically Black Colleges and Universities: A Narrative History, 1837-2009*. Reprint edition. Macon, GA: Mercer University Press, 2015.

Mellor, Philip A., and ChrisShilling. "Body Pedagogics and the Religious Habitus: A New Direction for the Sociological Study of Religion." *Religion*, 40, no. 1 (2010, January 1): 27–38. https://doi.org/10.1016/j.religion.2009.07.001

Mitchell, Travis. "Faith Among Black Americans." *Pew Research Center's Religion & Public Life Project* (blog), 2021, February 16. https://www.pewresearch.org/religion/2021/02/16/faith-among-black-americans/

Melvin Oliver and Thomas M. Shapiro, eds. *Black Wealth/White Wealth: A New Perspective on Racial Inequality*. 2nd ed. New York: Routledge, 2006.

Omi, Michael, and Howard, Winant. *Racial Formation in the United States*. 3rd ed. New York: Routledge, 2014.

Paris, Peter J. *The Social Teaching of the Black Churches*. Philadelphia, PA: Augsburg Fortress Publishers, 1998.

Peter J. Paris, Ed. *The Spirituality of African Peoples: The Search for a Common Moral Discourse*. Minneapolis, MN: Fortress Press, 1994.

Patterson, Orlando. "Authority, Alienation, and Social Death." In *African American Religious Thought: An Anthology*, edited by Cornel West, and Eddie S. Glaude Jr., 99–155. Louisville, KY: Westminster John Knox Press, 2003.

Patterson, Orlando. *Slavery and Social Death: A Comparative Study.* 1st ed. Cambridge, MA: Harvard University Press, 1982.

Pinn, Anthony B. "DuBois' Souls: Thoughts on 'Veiled' Bodies and the Study of Black Religion." *The North Star: A Journal of African American Religious History*, 6, no. 2 (Spring 2003): 1–5. https://www.princeton.edu/~jweisenf/northstar/volume6/pinn.html

Pinn, Anthony B. *Embodiment and the New Shape of Black Theological Thought.* New York: NYU Press, 2010.

Pinn, Anthony B. *Terror and Triumph.* Minneapolis, MN: Augsburg Fortress Publishers, 2003.

Pinn, Anthony B. *The End of God-Talk: An African American Humanist Theology.* Oxford; New York: Oxford University Press, 2012.

Smith, Jonathan Z. "Religion, Religions, Religious." In *Critical Terms for Religious Studies*, edited by Mark C. Taylor. Chicago: The University of Chicago Press, 1998.

Smith, Theophus H. *Conjuring Culture: Biblical Formations of Black America.* New York: Oxford University Press, 1995.

Tesfamariam, Rahiel. "Why the Modern Civil Rights Movement Keeps Religious Leaders at Arm's Length." *Washington Post*, September 18, 2015. https://www.washingtonpost.com/opinions/how-black-activism-lost-its-religion/2015/09/18/2f56fc00-5d6b-11e5-8e9e-dce8a2a2a679_story.html

Thurgood Marshall College Fund. "About HBCUs." Accessed September 30, 2023. https://www.tmcf.org/about-us/member-schools/about-hbcus/

Turner, Bryan S. *The Body and Society.* 3rd ed. Los Angeles, CA: SAGE Publications Ltd, 2008.

Turner, Victor W., Abrahams, Roger D., and Harris, Alfred. *The Ritual Process: Structure and Anti-Structure.* 1st ed. New York: Aldine Transaction, 1995.

CHAPTER 4

THE GOSPEL OF ASKING QUESTIONS

Melanye Price
Prairie View A&M University, USA

ABSTRACT

In this chapter, drawing on personal experience of returning to her under-graduate institution as a professor and administrator, the author explores the ways in which the language and symbols of her religious upbringing helped her see value in the "gospel of asking questions" as a basic framework for colle-giate pedagogy and practice. That is to say, the practice of critical engagement and examination provides tools necessary for creative insight and solutions to key challenges facing a troubled United States. The author ends the essay by suggesting curricular changes that enhance the educational process, in this case by celebrating the process of questioning.

Keywords: Critical engagement; Prairie View A&M University; intellectual life; white gaze; syllabi; skepticism

The notion of the gospel is multifaceted in Christian life. In its simplest form, we know it as the message spread by Christians that conveys the teach-ings of Jesus Christ. But the Christianity gospel has come to signify so much more. To say something is gospel is to imbue it with authority and integrity. If someone says they are telling you the "gospel truth," they are trying to

'Saving' Education, pages 75–87

doi:10.1108/978-1-83708-894-220251005

make clear both the veracity of the claim and the emphatic nature of the truth they are offering. Moreover, it is a truth that you should not bother questioning because the addition of gospel as an adjective has rendered it beyond doubt. Alternatively, the term gospel can simply represent a genre of music that is sung every Sunday in most Black churches. This is music that sets the tone and interacts with the dynamic nature of worship. It can push the worship experience to frenzied heights and lull the congregation into a peaceful repose. It is a signal of transition and the one signaling the valence of the transition.

Mindful of this, I suggest the following ideas benefit from being seen in this multifaceted way—as a mode of the gospel. Without question, I am certain that there must be greater space for students to do more questioning at historically Black colleges and universities (HBCUs). If HBCUs are to remain the training grounds for transformative leadership in the African American community, then asking questions and practicing skepticism must become the new pedagogical gospel of HBCU life.

A healthy dose of skepticism is the building block to training good scholars and good citizens. Skepticism is also a primary endeavor of any good mission driven HBCU. When most of these colleges were founded, nearly everyone except Black people were skeptical of the intellectual capacity of Black people. What began for some as a social experiment and for others as a form of social protest, HBCUs were formed to educate freed people and their descendants in order to populate professions necessary to create and maintain community. Though chattel slavery ended, racial segregation was cemented as the societal order. Over the years, possibilities for racial integration have expanded; yet, HBCUs continue to play an outsized role in African American higher education. In the Black Live Matter era the number of students seeking out HBCUs has significantly increase as they look for what they perceive as a safe harbor from increasing racial animus. In 2023, applications to HBCUs increased 30% and students often cited a hostile racial climate for their decision to choose an HBCU.[1]

In 2019, I returned to my alma mater, Prairie View A&M University, as professor in an endowed chair with the mandate to strengthen African American Studies (AFAM) across the curriculum. Nearly 30 years since I was a student there, both my theological and intellectual life have expanded (and hopefully matured). Though direct connections between churches and HBCUs are less visible in the contemporary moment, they remain quite similar in style and rhetoric.[2] To be honest, of all the things I have done in my 20-year career as an academic, being the chair of a Baptist church trustee board responsible for the church's facilities and fiscal management helped me as I returned to Prairie View more than anything else.

What I would like to offer here are a series of thoughts about my own relationship to religion vis-à-vis a religious upbringing, how my own theological leanings have shifted, and what it has meant for my return to teach at my alma mater. Much of this will focus on what I believe is the most important African American religious practices, which for these purposes I call the *gospel of asking questions*—i.e., the practice of deep examination of the "how and why" of life. I believe such a process of critical engagement will, hopefully, lead to new and transformative insights that serve as the precursor to developing solutions to key challenges.

REPAIRERS OF THE BREACH

In many ways I see HBCU faculty as empowering the repairers of the racial breach. I would add the heterosexist patriarchal white supremacist breach since much of the activism around these issues has been directly linked to and inspired by the legacy of civil rights advocacy by HBCUs—but, for this essay, at the very least the racial breach needs consideration. Since Reconstruction, HBCU faculty, students, and graduates have acted as political and cultural strategists and activists who have attempted to understand the pernicious and persistent nature of racism. They have worked to dismantle systems guided by white supremacy that have so adversely affected the lives of African descendant people. From their inception they have been hot-beds of activism and their students have been the foot soldiers in African American insurgent efforts.

It is also true that HBCUs historically have had very rigid views of what that preparation entails. You will note pictures of early HBCU students who were expected to mimic Victorian dress and values as a method of social assimilation and acceptance. The transition from enslavement to emancipation hadn't changed all hearts and minds about the capacity of African Americans to be full and equal citizens. Thus, early HBCU efforts were centered on disproving prevailing assumptions about African Americans through intellectual pursuits and strict adherence to Eurocentric behavioral norms. The critical component of preparation emphasized an unquestioning adherence to hierarchy and moral uprightness.

To an extent, these habituations are true today. Black colleges continue to be socializing agents in the lives of its students. Under the guise of preparing students for leadership in the larger world and, in some ways, protecting them from the outsized role race will play in their postundergraduate lives, Black colleges push all students to adhere to a kind of propriety that will be viewed positively by employers and the wider Black community. One overt example is a reliance on dress codes. Hampton University lists a student dress code on its website.[3] As recently as 2009, Morehouse instituted a new dress code policy and their Vice President of the Office of Student Engagement reflected on these dual impulses, noting, "we know the challenges that young African-American men face. We know that how a student dresses has nothing to do with what is in their head, but first impressions mean everything."[4] The politics of respectability remains at the forefront of considerations in how HBCUs train their students for life beyond their grounds.

Despite respectability norms and public statements regarding propriety, we know that many of the most transformational African American leaders who skirted and leaped over the lines of respectability were also trained on these campuses. In *Shelter in a Time of Storm: How HBCUs Fosters Generations of Leadership and Activism,* Jelani Manu-Gowon Favors has explained the emergence of generations of activists at HBCUs through their use of what he calls the second curriculum. In his estimation, faculty and staff at Black colleges stressed European intellectual traditions and middle-class norms and pushed students to understand the cannons of their disciplines and present themselves according to mainstream societal standards, but also regularly supplemented this training with strident critiques of those traditions. In addition, Black Colleges provided a liminal space for Black people to consider their own humanity and place in American society. The physical location, itself, set it apart from the white gaze and often hostile forces trying to exert pressure on Black life. In many cases, syllabi could not account for the critical nuances in how material was presented to students and auxiliary readings offered to students. As a result, HBCU students became activist because of what, where and how they were being taught in classrooms and other spaces not despite them.[5]

Our job as HBCU faculty and mentors of young impressionable students is to give them the space to be skeptical in the classroom. We make room for them to have the same privilege as their ancestors to study and know for themselves what they believe and how they will live out those beliefs. If there is a reason to "get back to the legacy," then the legacy to which we lead our students is the legacy of skepticism about the world around them and whether its current formation is one with which they can live. It is the urgent need to question everything, knowing that asking questions is a two-edge sword. Why? Because ultimately, the students will begin to use these same skills to question their professors and the power dynamics within your relationship.

RETURNING THE HUMAN TO BLACK COLLEGE MORAL AND INTELLECTUAL LIFE

Even HBCUs that emphasized agricultural and vocational training, offer humanities courses to all its students. History, literature, and other disciplines were a central feature of HBCU curricula. Favors notes that starting in the 1980s, many HBCUs (particularly land-grants) took a sharp turn away from the humanities and social scientists and toward Science, Technology, Engineering, and Mathematics.[6] A crucial example of this transition is that former Prairie View A&M University President Ruth Simmons and fashion icon and writer, Andre Leon Talley, both got degrees in French from HBCUs. However, French departments—along with some other language offerings—have largely disappeared from the HBCU landscape. The disappearance of humanities courses occurred for various reasons, but the fallout resulted in a retreat from disciplines that foster the practice of questioning in service to applied majors that have limited the spaces where students are trained to analyze and interrogate the world around them and imagine new frontiers. This deficit in the humanities also means that faculty who teach hard science-based courses work harder to instill skills needed to engage in critical inquiry that would have been supplied in now deleted courses with a more humanist or social scientific focus.

Given this curricular loss, I believe the other institutional pillar of the African American community—the Black Church—should serve as another site for practicing social inquiry—a space to learn to doubt received knowledge, to expect complicated narratives, to grapple with uncertainty, and to be animated by a desire to answer some questions. The goal is for students to be buoyed by an inner confidence to live within liminal spaces African Americans often occupy in American life, where questions remain unanswered and their own thoughts are the grounds for creating new terrains of African American liberation. From my perspective, engaging in a practice of skepticism and reimagining is the only explanation for Black adherence to Christianity post-Emancipation. At some point, enslaved Africans asked questions and wrestled with the texts offered them on Sunday mornings to create a more liberatory version—one allowing space for their humanity—than what they may have heard from slavers.

Yet for many of our students who are raised in the contemporary Black Church this possibility of an alternative space for skepticism is foreclosed because of the rigid theologies of many mainstream Black churches. The prominence of the prosperity gospel that is triumphant without question, along with the decision some make to partner with more conservative evangelical (read "white") churches means that many students now have had very little access to models of faith that include skepticism as a primary feature.[7] Indeed, they are much more likely to have been taught that questioning represents waning and weak faith. Further, they are taught that this lack of surety could explain a multitude of problems and downturns in their personal and professional lives.

MY JOURNEY TO A PRACTICE OF SKEPTICISM

By way of context, I began my early life in a church named Unity in God Missionary Baptist Church in southeast Houston (TX). In this church, women only wore skirts and women never spoke from the pulpit, while doing absolutely everything else—from raising money, to teaching Sunday School, to cooking communal meals, to cleaning the sanctuary. And though my mother questioned everything there and everywhere, the basic tenets of the faith of that church relied on accounts of unwavering faith as the answer to and diagnosis of personal and community problems. Individual piety insulated adherents from the troubles of the world—from what was variously referred to as "out there," "the streets," or "worldly" spaces.

When I was 14, I started attending Windsor Village United Methodist Church, a mega church where I encountered ministers with seminary degrees for the first time in my life. (I am not sure that I knew there was a formal study for ministers before that point.) I was fortunate enough to get there before the full impact of the prosperity gospel movement and what Charrise Barron calls the Platinum Age of Gospel.[8] At this mega church I heard preachers who were, I would later come to know, Womanist theologians. It was my first experience hearing Renita Weems, Valerie Bridgeman, Claudette Copeland and others preach. I learned that a Womanist faith is a questioning faith; it shirks easy or simplistic answers. In my eyes, it wrestles with God and the Biblical text, to find solutions and hope in a theological tradition that is filled with atrocities toward a host of minorities including women and queer folks. It ends sermons with more questions than it began with and leaves the people in the pews in a quandary rather than sheer euphoria. However, it also gives life and voice to the questions that have always been there and confronts them directly without deflections or panacea. It would be years before I would understand the gift of being exposed to a pedagogy of skepticism and allowed the space to ask challenge questions even if they shook the foundations of what I believed.

When I left home to attend an HBCU, I also stepped away from church at the same moment that mega churches began to lean heavily into nondenominationalism and embrace prosperity gospel and white evangelicalism—including the church that initially exposed me to Womanist theology. I was away from church for almost a decade. Much to my mother's joy, I returned to church at some point and began to embrace Black churches with a clear social justice and community outreach mission, with much less focus on denominational affiliations and more on the interplay of faith and works. My decision to affiliate was based on a simple principle, "If I can't tell what you are doing in your neighborhood, I don't want to attend." This principle led me to a Catholic church run by Jesuits priests in Columbus, Ohio, and a Black Baptist church lead by a Womanist pastor in Philadelphia. Both congregations, in their own way, made a stand in a community that most people with means and resources had long abandoned. This questioning journey, nurtured in these two disparate faith communities, expanded my faith but also made it impossible to go home to the mega church where I was raised. Now, the distance between the good work they did and the theology they espoused seemed too far from each other, and the distance between my current theology and that of my youth seemed too far to bridge.

GOSPEL MUSIC: THE SOUNDTRACK TO ASKING QUESTIONS

Gospel music asks a million questions and simultaneously admonishes doubters—at times in the same song! It is also the liturgical constant in most Black churches. It was played in the Baptist churches of my childhood and adulthood, the United Methodist Church of my youth, and the Catholic Church of my young adulthood. It is so important to my worship experience that I won't attend a church without it. Two gospel songs from my own childhood encapsulate what I see as a glaring dichotomy in Black religious life, but one that also spills into Black colleges.

The first song is by the Mississippi Mass Choir, produced by Malaco Record, called "When I Rose This Morning. "The lyrics start by saying, "This morning when I rose, I didn't have doubt…I didn't have no doubt that God will take care of me." So many similar gospel songs that espouse a kind of fixed or assured faith that things will somehow work out characterizes the kind of confidence based in a knowing faith that many students possess (or claim to possess) when I meet them. There are things they "just know" about life and Black people, in particular, that are deeply and rigidly held. And like the song, they repeat these beliefs about how the world works and how Black people fit into that world. When all the time my job is to inject the notion that just maybe evidence and your own experience suggest that doubt is warranted. In fact, healthy and necessary doubt is the first step to improving the psychological and material reality of their own communities. Doubt forces one to ask the past, "why?" and the future, "what?"

Difficulties arise because once one embraces doubt, new expansive worlds open up, and there is a strong possibility that one's religious understanding will overwhelm the kind of sure faith of my own Baptist and many of our religious upbringing. Such openings have the potential to radically alter student's relationships with their home church and communities, and their own families—which for many of them is an abiding fear. Because over 70% of HBCU students are Pell Grant eligible and 40% are first generation college students, they often leave home shrouded by angst and fear from their families and friends that they will come back unrecognizable. HBCU students return home more educated and financially successful than most members of their community of origin. Managing this transformation is a fraught process with concerns often openly expressed by friends and family.

And yet we professors press on and push them to begin questioning the things they know and encouraging them to seek out the unknown and question more. For example, in my Black Politics survey course we begin with the question, "how did the formerly enslaved structure their social and political world." We read Elsa Barkley Brown's "Negotiating and Transforming the Public Sphere"[9] that begins with church politics. In the story she recounts women petition to be able to vote in the First African

Baptist Church business meeting and readers learn that they are not asking for new rights but instead they are looking for the restoration of a right they once had. This article grounds the women's request in four important historical touchpoints: (1) Immediately after Emancipation, the first thing these newly freed citizens did was restore families and establish colleges and churches; (2) Men, women, *and* children participated in the decision-making process; (3) Participation was not and did not require an orderly performance of a monolithic politic; and (4) Mega churches in terms of numbers are not new and are not preternaturally conservative or apolitical.

Once this historical social and political order is established, the class has to start talking about why we perceive a male-centered political leadership style as the only choice in contemporary Black politics. Because if this leadership style is not an innate function of our political history, then any moves to challenge patriarchy and the singularity of political narratives are not anathema to Black culture and history. Instead in some ways, we can frame it as a way to return to the liberating vision of those newly freed citizens whose commitment to freedom was born out a clear understanding of what it meant to not have it. This means that for the rest of the course, everything else that students believe to be fact about Black political behavior can be interrogated. And it's the act of interrogating that I am trying to nurture. This article by Brown is helpful for many reasons but mostly because it resets our notions of Black institutions and leadership, and I am trying to get students to do both.

Beyond just breaking down a rigid faith, the goal of generative questioning is to foster an imagination that is augmented by more expansive, more progressive, and sometimes more accurate and research-based views of even their own history. In addition, we give students the desire and skills to do good research so that they are empowered for the rest of their lives to ask questions, look for evidence, and begin to formulate answers.

The other song from my childhood is "The Question Is," by The Winans. In this song, rather than repeatedly attesting to a doubtless faith, this song is a litany of questions: "Will I ever leave you; Will I do his will; When will Jesus return…," and it goes on.[10] In some ways, this is the kind thinking that I am pushing students toward, where the world is more questions and curiosity than surety and fixity of idea. My role is to help them accept that there is more unknown than known realities, especially because the known worlds they come from are filled with structured inequalities. The answers to the questions the Winans pose require a simple yes or no; but to adhere to the theology I've spoken of, the questions are never all yeses or all noes. The answer can be different, yet support the same position. Thus, this song is also a methodological example of the need to ask multivalent questions that require the investigator to consider various sides of the problem and question all sides.

Ultimately this song provides answers to its own questions; however, it is the very act of questioning that make it important. The song asks questions so as to define the relationship between the vocalist and God, and to illustrate faithfulness. It is a clear attempt to understand the structure of that relationship. In American life, we tend to see structures as immutable, and the long view of history coupled with a liberated imagination can change the most immutable structure. Black peoples' sojourn in the Americas is a testament to the ability to create opportunities for and demand changes. Questions help break through the seeming immutability.

TAILORING THIS GOSPEL TO HBCU STUDENTS

Up to this point, much of this could be true for any student not just students at HBCUs. All universities should foster an atmosphere of questioning and curiosity and teach sound research and investigative skills.

So how might HBCU students need greater (or more tailored) prodding toward skepticism? First, like the larger African American community, HBCU students are often more religious than other students and certainly engage in more religious rhetoric. High levels of religiosity remain a key feature of community life on HBCU campuses while students are simultaneously engaged in a process of world expansion. For many HBCUs, religious life centers around a campus chapel that functions as a Protestant church, where the chaplain largely serves as its pastor.[11] Thus, educators must contend with the nature of that religiosity. Students who were born in this millennia, live in many ways with a different Black Church than the one in which I was raised. For example, they largely have no experience of line singing and testimonial services, yet the Black church's tradition of patriarchy and performance of piety remain. Our goal should be to get them to see the societal structures that uphold traditions and rewards particular performances.

Second, it is important to acknowledge that many Black students have been socialized in a culture that tells them that to be respectful is to *not* ask questions and *not* challenge. They have been taught to believe that to seek clarification, to refute positions, or to attempt to correct your behaviors is a betrayal of the affections and hard work of your elders. Clinging to these traditions, makes it more difficult to get students to hold steady in spaces of doubt and to see process and the structural forces at play. At some level, Black parents, other elders in their community, and HBCU leadership rely on these engrained teachings that produce the performance of respectfulness to maintain order. They rely on it because they are a part of this same culture and believe it, and because it is useful to them. The conditioning takes the form of a rigid either/or social order where students, faculty and staff are either respectful or not, or well-behaved or not. To end up in the "not" category puts one out of not just social bounds but also the bounds of communal acceptance, and can sometimes determine who gets institutional support. I have begun to focus on this particular aspect of HBCU life more regularly in my work to bring a Bachelor of Arts in African and AFAM to Prairie View.

AFAM has its beginning in a space of skepticism and asking questions. With its activist origins, AFAM's primary question stems from a desire to understand the history and contemporary life of Black people as a method of strategizing about future liberation. This requires critical questions of every academic cannon and skepticism of all the conclusions they have drawn. It centers itself around the basic question of where the African diaspora fits into the process of historical recovery and knowledge production. Now, more than 1,200 institutions country-wide have an AFAM department, program or center. The first program was started in 1968 at San Francisco State College, as several fields of study arose in the shadow of the Civil Rights and Women's Rights movements.[12] Many departments have celebrated their 50th anniversary in the last few years. When I told people who have been in this work for years what I had come home to do, the reactions ranged from disbelief that we did not already have it, to an assumption of backwardness. Frankly, it was unclear to *me* why so few HBCUs had established AFAM Programs.

HBCU students helped birth the 1960s Civil Rights Movement and engaged in campus protests like many students across the country. But it wasn't until I was asked to help formulate a program that I asked more questions. Both HBCUs and predominantly white campuses were sites of large-scale student protests in the 1960s and 1970s, but the outcome of and the motivations for those protests were somewhat different. Martha Biondi points out that demands by HBCU students were far more expansive than on other campuses. Beyond curricular changes and diversifying faculty ranks, HBCU students were asking for changes in legislative funding schemes, more say in university governance, and improved infrastructure. They were seeking redress for years of disinvestment that had left their campus buildings badly worn. Because predominantly white campuses were simultaneously attempting to respond to societal demands of more integration, they needed to respond to student protests by demonstrating a certain amount of openness. As a result, they established African American or Ethnic Studies programs and hired more Black faculty members. The response to student protests as HBCUs were decidedly more violent and lethal than Black student protests on predominantly white campuses. National guardsmen fired into campus buildings and at student protestors. Student leaders and empathetic faculty members were expelled from campuses.[13] The lesson learned by many HBCU administrators, faculty and students was clear. This is not to suggestion that HBCU students did not continue to engage in protests and push for change—they did. However, it also meant that the expectations and performance of respectability was more deeply inscribed into the culture.

What was clear during the student campus protests is that HBCU students pinpointed the structural influences within higher education and politics that impeded their ability to receive fully benefits of a college education. Before they launched their movement, they asked questions about how their campuses came to entail unequal conditions and searched for answers beyond individual behavior and other deficit models. While it took court cases and federal intervention to even receive a portion of what HBCUs deserved, there would be nothing gained if the students had not been skeptical of the durability of their conditions and initiated a series of questions about how their reality could be transformed.

Learning to question, and embracing skepticism, encourages students to see systems rather than individual behavior as the source of community problems and then set about transforming those systems. For these reasons, I force my students to question; I walk with them in spaces of doubt; I refrain from offering the ways I have resolved uncertainty; and I help them learn to assess sources and read between the lines of the text to analyze what is omitted as much as what is asserted. I try to help them see that bigger worldviews can coexist with our communities of origin. I reassure them that they will not be alone in their skepticism. I assure them that in the same way that I found new communities where questioning the things we do is nurtured and encouraged, I am sure they can find the same.

More than anything I tell them, they must ask more questions, challenge societal order, and transform the lived environment because we—the generations ahead of them and behind them—are counting on them to do it. And then we read humanities and social science scholars who provide accounts of the myriad ways our ancestors have done the same and won. I implore them to imagine the uncertainty of the first students on our campus who had all been born enslaved and arrived on the grounds of a former plantation to be educated. What kinds of questions must they have asked as they studied, ate, and slept in a house where slavers once lived—a house that remained in use for half a century or more. I make clear that by entering an HBCU campus they have taken on the birthright and obligation to never accept the society they were born into as the final word on the matter. In short, I spread the gospel of asking questions because without questions there is no path to greater progress.

NOTES

1. Joyce E. Davis, "HBCUs See Surge in Applications After George Floyd Protests, Help From Black Celebs." https://www.usatoday.com/story/news/2023/02/18/more-students-apply-historic-black-colleges-and-universities/11155356002/
2. Many HBCUs maintain religious affiliations. Some more overt like Oakwood College in Alabama (Seventh Day Adventist) Xavier University (Catholic) or

Virginia Union University (Baptist). There are others who still retain historical relations and some measure of funding from religious denominations.
For instance, the United Methodist Church has a Black College Fund that
supports the largest number of Black colleges of any denomination and that
distributes funds to 11 HBCUs including Clark Atlanta, Bennett and Rusk.

3. Here is a link to Hampton University's website about its dress code: https://
home.hamptonu.edu/activities/dress-code/. In recent years, students have
protested about various problems at Hampton including its dress code
(https://www.theroot.com/the-mutiny-at-hampton-university-1823431651).

4. Mishaun Simon, "Morehouse Dress Code Seeks to 'Get Back to the Legacy'."
Atlanta Journal Constitution, Local News (2009). https://www.ajc.com/news/
local/morehouse-dress-code-seeks-get-back-the-legacy/4BQeGNx4kTckXgx
mlUaJnN/

5. Jelani Manu-Gowon Favors, *Shelter in a Time of Storm: How Black Colleges Fostered
Generations of Leadership and Activism* (Chapel Hill: University of North Carolina Press, 2019).

6. Ibid.

7. Tamelyn N. Tucker-Worgs, *The Black Mega Church: Theology, Gender, and the Politics of Public Engagement* (Waco, TX: Baylor University Press, 2012).

8. Charrise Barron, *The Platinum Age of Gospel: Contemporary Gospel Since the 1990s*
(forthcoming).

9. Elsa Barkley Brown, "Negotiating and Transforming the Public Sphere: African American Political Life in the Transition from Slavery to Freedom." *Public
Culture,* 7, no. 1 (1994): 107–46.

10. The Winans, "The Question Is," Introducing, Light Records, 1981.

11. In a 2018 article in *Diverse Issues in Higher Education,* the author discusses the
changing nature of HBCU chaplain positions at HBCUs but simply focuses
(https://www.diverseeducation.com/demographics/african-american/arti-
cle/15103862/hbcu-chaplains-evolve-to-meet-the-spiritual-needs-of-their-stu-
dents).

12. Erin Blakemore, "The Origins of African American Studies, Explained," *National Geographic,* February 13, 2023. https://www.nationalgeographic.com/histo-
ry/article/african-american-black-studies-origins-explained#:~:text=The%20
first%20ethnic%20studies%20program,War%20movement%20in%20
the%20area

13. Martha Biondi, *The Black Revolution on Campus* (Los Angeles: The University
of California Press, 2014).

REFERENCES

Barron, Charrise. *The Platinum Age of Gospel: Contemporary Gospel Since the 1990s*
(under review).

Biondi, Martha. *The Black Revolution on Campus.* Los Angeles: The University of California Press, 2014.

Blakemore, Erin. "The Origins of African American Studies, Explained." *National
Geographic* (2023, February 13).

Brown, Elsa Barkley. "Negotiating and Transforming the Public Sphere: African American Political Life in the Transition from Slavery to Freedom." *Public Culture* 7, no. 1 (1994): 107–46.

Favors, Jelani Manu-Gowon. *Shelter in a Time of Storm: How Black Colleges Fostered Generations of Leadership and Activism.* Chapel Hill: University of North Carolina Press, 2019.

Simon, Mishaun. "Morehouse Dress Code Seeks to 'Get Back to the Legacy'." *Atlanta Journal Constitution,* October 17, 2009. https://www.ajc.com/news/local/morehouse-dress-code-seeks-get-back-the-legacy/4BQeGNx4kTckXgx mlUaJnN/

Tucker-Worgs, Tamelyn N. *The Black Mega Church: Theology, Gender, and the Politics of Public Engagement* (Waco, TX: Baylor University Press, 2012).

CHAPTER 5

"WE'VE COME THIS FAR BY FAITH!": OUR PAST, PURPOSE & POWER

Cecil Andrew Duffie
Julius S. Scott, Sr. Chapel, USA

ABSTRACT

The author gives priority to the voices of those working on historically Black colleges and universities (HBCU) campuses with an explicit charge to maintain a religious orientation and provide spiritual counsel—e.g., Deans of the Chapel and chaplains. Using a social science informed methodology, the author argues religion is at the core of HBCUs' self-understanding as reflected in their mottos and guiding principles, and as advanced by leaders responsible for the religious and spiritual well-being of those higher education communities. By highlighting the voices of figures doing the work, the author aims to describe the manner in which issues of identity are worked out through engagement with a religiously motivated vocabulary and grammar of life.

Keywords: Chaplains; spiritual counsel; Dean of Chapel; methodology; advocacy; pastoral care

'Saving' Education, pages 89–110
Copyright © 2025 by Emerald Publishing Limited
doi:10.1108/978-1-83708-894-220251006

The Pentecostal-reared songwriter and church musician Albert A. Goodson pinned these words in 1956:

> We have come this far by faith,
>
> Leaning on the Lord,
>
> Trusting in God's Holy Word,
>
> This Lord has never failed us yet.[1]

In many ways, these lyrics epitomize the essence of Black religious and spiritual life leaders serving America's historically Black colleges and universities (HBCUs). Although faith has long been recognized as one of the foundations of higher education in America, religion has always been central to the foundation of Black higher education and indeed, crucial in the establishment and growth of HBCUs.

When considering HBCUs one can immediately note the mottos that have guided these institutions. Mottos constitute an institution's values and help to provide meaning as well as the ideals and beliefs espoused in their founding. Mottos help to define mission. John Thelin wrote of the early American education institutions and said of mottos that "there is a touching sense of high purpose in them...admirable voices crying out in the New World wilderness, looking for light and truth - and not without strong Christian faith combined with secular resolve." He later called them "noble purposes."[2] Similar sentiments are evident in the mottos, and thus the missions of the top six HBCUs in the country, as ranked by *US News & World Report* in 2022:

> Howard University: *Truth and Service*; Morehouse College: *And There Was Light*; Spelman College: *Our Whole School for Christ*; Hampton University: *The Standard of Excellence, An Education for Life*; Xavier University of Louisiana: *With God's Help There Is Nothing to Fear*; and Tuskegee University: *Knowledge, Leadership, Service*.

Of the six HBCUs, two have mottos or missions directly linked to religious practice, while the other four espouse strong moral and ethical ambitions. It is my argument that Black religious and spiritual life leaders are the primary propagators of these aims, as they are tasked with the spiritual, religious, and ethical dimensions of leadership on the campus.

When contemplating religion and HBCUs (history, mission, and impact), understanding the role of Black religious and spiritual life leaders helps to make meaning, thus providing context, for Black leadership in higher education. This qualitative study utilizing narrative inquiry examines the lived experiences of Black religious and spiritual life leaders (deans, chaplains, directors of religious life, and directors of spiritual life) at HBCUs and seeks to place their past, purpose, and power in their own historical and personal context.[3] The research question for the study is: How do Black religious and spiritual life leaders share narratives of: Black identity, the interaction of race and gender, and leadership and mission?

As a qualitative researcher, let me be clear from the outset about my positionality. I have a passion for interfaith and spiritual engagement on college campuses. In offices of the dean of the chapel specifically, or within college and university chaplaincy more broadly, I have found a commitment to empowering leadership development and engaging the global community, while also promoting interfaith dialog and cooperation that help students gain a deepened understanding and respect for diverse faiths and cultures. I see effective interfaith and spiritual engagement as successful acts of involvement that create mutual respect. Conversations on how college campuses are expanding interfaith and spiritual activities are cutting-edge and drawing increased attention from students, faculty, staff, and administrators. I challenge the narrative of tolerance and push for a foundation and programming that requires real knowledge and trust of the other.

I approach this work with an obsession for the marriage of education and faith, an enthusiasm for Black religious history, and an excitement for the future of college and university chaplaincy. These emotions are driven by my assumption that Black religious and spiritual life leaders are crucial to the vitality of higher education and essential to the pathways that will move the discipline forward.

It is crucial to review some of the pertinent literature on religion in higher education broadly and in HBUCs specifically, before addressing the history of religious and spiritual life leaders and their contribution to the landscape of higher education. Critical information about religion in higher education and its leaders has long been studied and analyzed. I seek to summarize that work here to give grounding and basis to the past.

OUR PAST

Higher education in America had its foundation in religion.[4] In the 1600s, when colleges and universities were first birthed in the United States, they were training grounds for White Protestant clergyman.[5] The very idea of college and university chaplaincy and campus ministry was conceived through religious societies at Harvard College as early as the 18th century.[6] Interest in religious and spiritual life and its function within higher education have been widely shared within higher education literature.[7] Of the Ivy League schools, it is notable that all have a prominent, dedicated religious edifice or chapel. Harvard University has Harvard Memorial Church; Yale University has University Church (Battell Chapel); Princeton University has Princeton University Chapel (Marquand Chapel); Columbia University has

St. Paul's Chapel; Brown University has Manning Chapel; Dartmouth College has Rollins Chapel; and Cornell University has Sage Chapel. Unlike the other colonial-era schools with religious affiliations (Brown – Baptist; Harvard – Congregationalist; Columbia and Yale – Anglican), even the non-sectarian University of Pennsylvania has a Main Chapel.[8]

Religion has also always been at the helm of Black higher education, especially at HBCUs. Most HBCUs have the distinction of being formed during the Reconstruction period through the end of the 19th century.[9] While these spaces morphed into safe havens for students and surrounding communities, they originally had the sole responsibility of educating freed Blacks, and in some cases, former slaves. Roebuck and Murty wrote that even though some Northern Whites discouraged Blacks from gaining an education, some missionary societies countered and created colleges and schools for Blacks' development.[10] Still, scholars have debated why such institutions were founded, questioning the real motives behind White philanthropy and whether Blacks who attended southern agricultural institutions were doomed to the plague of Black peasantry.[11] As a matter of fact, northerners who came from missionary societies went to the South with the idea of seeking to "civilize" Blacks, who they perceived were so pummeled by enslavement and need northerners' guidance.[12]

Whites' rationale did not stop Black church groups, including the African Methodist Episcopal Church, the Colored Methodist Episcopal Church, and the African Methodist Episcopal Zion Church, from creating HBCUs. These Methodists denominations, founded not due to ecclesial differences but in protest of unequal treatment of race, created transformational church schools. These schools, including colleges and universities, were founded in order to replicate and perpetuate Christian doctrine, faith and learning. Anderson explained that:

> A significant number of black secondary schools and colleges were organized and controlled by black religious organizations. The African Methodist Episcopal church, the Colored Methodist Episcopal church, and the African Methodist Episcopal Zion church established nearly all of the major colleges controlled by black organizations, and their combined voice largely articulated the educational policy of the black community.[13]

In addition to the Methodist denominations, the Baptist-affiliated American Missionary Association from 1861 to 1870 founded a dozen "normal schools" (i.e., teacher colleges) and seven other Black colleges.[14] Others were initiated by the American Baptist Home Mission Society, the Freedmen's Aid Society of the Methodist Episcopal Church, the Presbyterian Board of Missions, and Congregationalist churches.[15] It is clear that these schools had strong religious roots related to their founding. It is notable to mention that most HBCUs are in the Southeast where slavery was most prevalent.

Within these Black institutions were religious institutions known as chapels and memorial churches. Of the top six HBCUs in the country (as ranked by *US News & World Report*, 2022), all currently have such designations: Howard University has the Andrew Rankin Memorial Chapel; Morehouse College has the Martin L. King, Jr. International Chapel; Spelman College has the Sisters Chapel; Hampton University has The Memorial Church; Xavier University of Louisiana has St. Katharine Drexel Chapel; and Tuskegee University has Tuskegee University Chapel. In a history of Spelman College, former president Florence Read gave credence to Sisters Chapel as the central place for spiritual formation but also the bind uniting the entire institution through services and convocations. From the perspective of a faculty member, it was written:

Tying together the entire program of the departments at Spelman are the chapel services, convocations, and other religious services. They have always been a central feature of the college life – Spelman's 'spiritual classroom' they have been called; but never has to influence seem so earnestly and soberly received as now…The comfort of an organ prelude; or completely; the encouragement of the old, stalwart hymns; messages of a profound value in establishing that inner calm that is beyond the defeat of enemies; prayer-in such unforgettable moments of communication grows the creative dynamo which shall justify all this anguish, the understanding soul.[16]

Furthermore, in his history of Howard University, Rayford Logan noted the events and student body participation during Men's Glee Club and Women's Glee Club performances, as well as the "The Seven Last Words of Christ" service, were all held in the Chapel.[17] Though religion in Black higher education was central to its foundation and has been perpetuated through institutional functions such as memorial churches and chapels, the influence of religious and spiritual life programs on campus remains current. Notable HBCU programs and events including convocations, commencement, homecoming, the Martin Luther King Jr. holiday, and religious emphasis week have numerous religious and spiritual influences.[18] Cherry et al. wrote that HBCU programming also emerges from the office of the religious and spiritual life leader.[19] Morehouse's Martin Luther King Chapel notes its work in today's world:

Through transformative, moral cosmopolitan programs, the chapel serves as a center for the perpetuation of the evolutionary values of cosmopolitan spiritual ethics, nonviolence, service, and harmony in everyday life. Inspired by the possibility of the Beloved World Economic Community as the ethical meaning of the Presence of God, the Chapel embraces those who seek to make King's dream real as nonviolent creators of a sustainable world in which all people embody their spiritual magnificence by living with a commitment to unconditional love, responsibility, and justice.[20]

Ethical dimensions of leadership, especially surrounding service-learning and programming like "Alternative Spring Break", originate in the office of the religious and spiritual life leader, as confirmed by programs of the Andrew Rankin Memorial Chapel of Howard University. Service-learning, an important component of college and university chaplaincy, connects various pieces of the campus. Bernard L. Richardson, dean of the Andrew Rankin Memorial Chapel, lifted such a point in that "[Alternative Spring Break] is unique in that, over the years, all aspects of the University come together." Howard went on to describe its impact by noting:

> This year, Howard University Alternative Spring Break (HUASB) accepted its largest cohort in its history, tripling its size and growing its footprint both domestically and internationally. From the DMV to Puerto Rico, Detroit to Ghana, nearly 1,200 students embarked on a weeklong journey across 25 sites to address key issues regarding inequity and social justice.[21]

Howard University's program is a demonstration of what happens today within campus ministry which is associated with the very founding of higher education institutions. While religion was largely responsible for the founding of private colonial schools and many private HBCUs, there are other contemporary examples of religious and spiritual life offices in state colleges and universities, both in predominantly White institutions and at public HBCUs. The state-run University of Southern Indiana (USI) has a director of religious life who reports to the associate provost of student affairs and is employed by the Evansville Catholic Dioceses. The director of religious life, a full member of the staff of USI, handles day-to-day operations and gives spiritual direction to the entire community of staff, faculty, and students about places to worship and about personal concerns such as maintaining spiritual discipline. North Carolina Central University, which is a public HBCU, houses an office of spiritual dialog and development that offers guidance to students regarding their faith, spirituality, and ethics. Recent emphasis has been on the interfaith collaboration of interfaith dialogue.

While it is clear in the literature, the purpose of campus ministry and college and university chaplaincy, the leaders of this discipline have also been explored by means of various, more focused, research projects. Related to such work, in 2012, Threlfall-Holmes and Newitt wrote that a religious and spiritual life leader is one who is responsible for helping and shepherding people through change and evolution.[22] The idea of transition stretches across settings, especially when considering higher education.

The study of religious and spiritual life leaders has long been part of higher education literature.[23] One of the earliest works on religious and spiritual leaders was compiled by the Department of Religion in Higher Education at Yale Divinity School and consisted of a 250-response piece from clergy on their experiences at colleges. Rossman wrote specifically on the morale at particular institutions.[24] In 1964, Hammond described lived experiences from more than 1,000 campus clergypersons in the mid-20th century, almost four centuries after higher education came to existence in the United States.[25] Four years later, Hadden added to the early historical narrative of campus clergy as he reviewed how Protestant ministers interacted and were called to specific campuses around the country.[26] This work became a handbook of sorts, documenting best practices and ways to serve college and universities. An autobiographical account of Ernest Gordon, the university chaplain of Princeton, written around the same time as these formative studies, also gave an insider perspective to the role of a religious and spiritual life leader.[27]

More recent studies of religious and spiritual life leaders have been produced by various scholars. These recent studies have attempted to have religious and spiritual life leaders describe their own actions in their own voices. In 2004, Davis et al. examined denominational liaisons, chaplains, and campus ministers.[28] Their study detailed how religious and spiritual life leaders described their positions, spaces on campus, connection to other entities on campus, and the religious atmosphere. A study by Schmalzbauer, sponsored by the National Study of Campus Ministries, had 1,659 participants, with a subset of 335 religious and spiritual life leaders.[29] The first study of its kind since the 1950s postwar era, this research captured the addition of women in the field (up to 46% of all college chaplains) and Black religious and spiritual leaders (5% of all college chaplains). It important to mention that this 2018 study was a concentration of religious and spiritual leaders from primarily Christian institutions.

Barton et al. added to the literature with research focusing on how religious and spiritual life leaders contribute to the life of their institutions.[30] The themes that emerged from this study on the assets and proficiencies religious and spiritual life leaders bring to higher education included building bridges, building community, and tending to the soul of the university. Studies like this are especially crucial because of the explicit and intentional addition of participants from different faith traditions. Unlike previous studies by Davis in 2004 and Schmalzbauer in 2014, the 2020 study by Barton et al. made contributions to the literature regarding religious and spiritual life leaders who had previously been excluded. These researchers' key objective was to bring other voices into the literature, including participants from Unitarian, Hindu, Buddhist, Muslim, and Jewish faith traditions. Significantly, however, they deliberately chose to omit any specification of racial identity for the participants in the study. It is important to note that, despite such studies, there is scant information on the experiences of Black religious and spiritual life leaders in the current literature.

My goal here has been to go from a very board perceptive on the founding of some of America's earliest institutions, to the religious founding of many HBCUs, and then to demonstrate how this purpose is still perpetuated

through campus religious and spiritual life. Before introducing the qualitative findings, it is important to offer some information concerning the
perspective of existing literature on their role.

PURPOSE

The first Black Dean of Chapel was Howard Thurman, who held this
newly created position at Howard University. According to research by
Mark S. Giles, this job title and office had only existed at two other institutions, Princeton University and the University of Chicago.[31] The Dean
of Chapel, Giles says, represented a high-ranking title aligned with the
duties once performed by college presidents. These dean positions, once
created, typically answered directly to the president. This example aside,
to understand the function of the religious and spiritual life leader it is
important to explain their origin. In the late 1800s, colleges began to
hire nonclergymen as presidents.[32] The traditional duties were thereby
divided, creating a vacuum to be filled by clergymen with other titles such
as Campus Minister and Director of Religious Life. Giles notes that the
role of the Dean of Chapel was to provide leadership for the religious
life of the university, help shape a sense of community, manage the chapel building and supervise its staff, perform Sunday sermons, coordinate
chapel guest speakers, serve as campus minister in matters of advisement,
conduct annual and special ceremonies (orientations, marriages, funer-
als, etc.), and act as a liaison between the campus and community in matters of religion. The position also served as a historic link to the founding
principles of colleges and universities as a means to advance existing institutional efforts to promote the overall religious and spiritual life of the
immediate and surrounding community.

In 2013, Forster-Smith compiled an exploration of college and university chaplains in American higher education, including some 15 stories of
the lived experiences of leaders of religious and spiritual life offices.[33] This
project's purpose was to provide the first-ever interfaith resource for campus ministry. While it was quite detailed, the voices were primarily from
the perspective of predominately White institutions. The only HBCU Black
experience came from Gail Bowen, who shared her personal story of being
the university chaplain at Dillard University during and after Hurricane
Katrina as practical advice to other college and university chaplains.

And, in 2017, Faison used the case study method for a dissertation
focused on campus religious and spiritual life leaders.[34] Participants in five
interviews shared their perspectives on how such leaders can be relevant
in the current context of college and university chaplaincy. Interviewees
were religious and spiritual leaders who had served from 3 to 23 years.

Findings of this study were organized into themes such as the leaders' changing roles, their perceptions of their responsibilities, their preaching, and their programming.

Each of these two studies depicts the past and, in fact, offers little to address the need for viewing religious and spiritual life leaders' experiences through a varied group of participants with an emphasis on Black identity. Scholars including McKittrick and Mustaffa note the limited presence and the lack of Black experiences in the literature as erasure. For this reason, I am adamant about the need for research about Black religious and spiritual life leaders, their purpose and power. And in this way, I refute any innuendos of inferiority, oppression, and subjugation in the field, as the literature has been dominated by White voices. It is my belief that the stories and experiences offered in this essay help fill a gap in the existing literature. I am certain these findings offer greater understanding of these leaders highlights the manner in which diversity figures into religious leadership on campuses as well as serving to present the experiences of Black women, who are often left out and/or marginalized. As a liberationist, I promote the notion that we must continue to find alternative views to conservative and reactionary voices. After all, liberation is not simply for the text to free the people, but for the people to free the text.

The participants in the study included ten current Black religious and spiritual life leaders at selected institutions. Listed under their pseudonyms, they include:

The Reverend Brown, Dr. Cookman, Dr. Fisk, Dean Hampton, Pastor Howard,
Dean Paine, Dr. Smith, Dr. Washington, The Reverend Waters, and Dean Wiley.

These Black religious and spiritual life leaders at HBCUs consider their purpose to be a combination of advocacy, pastoral care, institutional support, and leading individuals to theological reflection. There were also undertones of gender related dynamics that prove to be important to mention. Of the six HBCUs noted earlier, in what follows, I would like to connect four mottos to how Black religious and spiritual life leaders at HBCUs see their purpose and one motto to note the dynamics of how gender played a role: Advocacy: "Truth and Service" (Howard University); Pastoral Care: "With God's Help There Is Nothing to Fear" (Xavier University of Louisiana); Institutional Support: "The Standard of Excellence, An Education for Life" (Hampton University); Leading Individuals to Theological Reflection: "And There Was Light" (Morehouse College); and Defining Gender Dynamics: "Knowledge, Leadership, Service" (Tuskegee University).

ADVOCACY: "TRUTH AND SERVICE"

Howard University's motto, "Truth and Service" is in line with how Black religious and spiritual life leaders see their work. Dean Hampton, considers himself an advocate and champion for issues of social justice and good. He said:

> My whole program is built on what it means to be a co-creator of the beloved world community…… That's got significant implications because of every issue, social issue, justice issue, climate issue that we're dealing with. The problem with most people, whether you are spiritually aware or not, or institution-ally identified or aligned with a particular faith tradition or denomination is that everybody's address is too small. That's why we can't deal effectively with climate change, global warming, global disaster, because we don't feel any the obligation to be responsible for the effect we're having because we're so disconnected from nature, we don't think we have any effect.

Dean Wiley not only attended an HBCU, but now works at an HBCU. She noted:

> I would say that I feel very privileged, because I work in an [HBCU], and I'm surrounded by very powerful Black women, Black women who are more power-ful than me, and I feel like it's a privilege in this regard. Sometimes it can get messy, let's be clear. I'm not going to paint a picture. Sometimes it can get messy, but the privilege in it is that I don't feel like my power threatens anybody to the extent that my life is miserable, and the times where I felt like I did have that experience at my job, I felt like I had recourse, I felt like I had resources, and I felt like as long as I tapped into my courage and I spoke up for myself, I was going to see a change, and it did happen because I work in a place that honors Black women, right? That wasn't always my story, however, and so I know what it feels like to feel very vulnerable, to feel very unprotected, to feel very tokenized.

INSTITUTIONAL SUPPORT: "THE STANDARD OF EXCELLENCE, AN EDUCATION FOR LIFE"

Hampton University espouses the idea that they are the standard of excel-lence—an education for life. This is in line with what Dr. Fisk said regarding how he not only counsel's students but the entire community and has the reach of the president. He mentioned:

> And so, I serve as a confidant to the president as much as I do to any other student or faculty member. And I've counseled people through divorces and

crises of all kinds. I was able to call the president and say, "Look, I need to talk to you. I think something critical is going on." And I could walk into his office. He calls me all the time. Calls me way more than I cared for him too. And sometimes he shows up in my office. And every president that I've been under since I've been in this position has literally sat at my desk in this office and voiced their displeasures, weaknesses, fears, all of it.

Reverend Waters agreed. She opened up about her institutional responsibility. She proclaimed:

So, I feel like my ease with people and my gentleness allows me to do some back channeling and to be perhaps in spaces that a chaplain isn't traditionally....I see myself in this role as making space and room for the next person. And if that next person is a woman who wants to pray at the cabinet meeting, then I want her to have that opportunity if she feels that she needs that. And so, I'm working on making the role more clear.

Dr. Cookman made mention of his experience working with the campus president, another connection to the excellence by which chaplains serve. He explained:

Several people said, "I don't know how this college is going to make it without you." Because now in the cabinet meetings, I can talk to the president, and sometimes I say things that's just, "Maybe I shouldn't have said that." But they get me, I've become the president's pastor and that has been a critical piece. Not only pastor to the college, but to the president himself or herself, herself in this instance, and I've always tried to maintain that posture everywhere I've gone.

Dr. Fisk also emphasized the connection, from the president to the custodians, mentioning how the Black religious and spiritual life leader can serve as an advisor to various offices. He revealed:

I've always considered myself a confidant. A confidant to every single president. And I think it's my role as a spiritual leader to let them know when even they are stepping out of their bounds. Sometimes they don't like me when I say it. I mean, [President] and I had a conversation in her conference room and I told her the same thing. I said, "You're too accessible. They think you are their friend. And when you get ready to give a directive, you're going to have a hard time doing that because they don't want their friend to be telling them what to do." We had a custodian here who was shot 10 times last summer. And so, I went over and had all the custodians called together and we prayed right there in the parking lot. And so, I consider myself the chaplain to everybody, not just students. I'm the chaplain to everybody. I'm the religious leader to everybody. I'm the spiritual leader for everybody on campus. That was not this role when I took it.

Reverend Waters understands her role to open the perspective of what voices needed to be heard in institutional settings. Her story questioned the role of empowering various campus constituents. She shared:

How do you care for a community who maybe needs to hear a certain voice that isn't your own, but also live in the authority that God has given you in this place, in this moment? And so that's a balance and I'm still trying to learn and walk. I understand it as a role that empowers people. I shouldn't be the only prayer. I am constantly in prayer for [HBCU], for our president, for… this week, especially I'm praying for the members of the Honors College. So I'm constantly in prayer and praying with my people. But I am not doing my work and I don't feel I'm doing what God called me to do if when we need a prayer, I'm the only one who can deliver it. And I know that that's really a fine line when my role in the institution is to be the prayer.

PASTORAL CARE: "WITH GOD'S HELP THERE IS NOTHING TO FEAR"

Dr. Fisk alludes to what Xavier University of Louisiana offers as its motto and made it a pastoral care ethic: With God's Help There Is Nothing to Fear. He shared a tragic story of the loss of a student and the Black religious and spiritual life leader's institutional responsibility to shepherd the community to a place of healing. He recounted:

Two years ago, we had two young men who were killed on our campus. And so, here you've got students standing around with dead bodies and blood and dah, dah, dah, dah, and shock across the campus. And I spent about the next 48 hours just trying to go to classrooms, pray with people, find out what the administration was doing. And one time, my role was positive as a male to be able to speak to young men and say, this is wrong and we've got to grow from this. I had to go into every single dormitory, male or female, and have a conversation about this thing that happened. The young ladies were mourning deeply. I mean, you had students who stood over that spot every day for weeks and months, really. I would go by there on my way to a meeting somewhere and there's a student standing there on that bloody spot. And matter of fact, when they tried to clean it up, the students protested and almost got violent about it. I had to tell the admin, "Give them time. Don't touch the spot."

Reverend Waters' remarked how she counsels students with the idea to make space for more. She noted:

… just thinking about my students that I've met and the things that I have observed in them, there is this fear almost of trying new things. As if… for example, I asked my students to create a TikTok video introducing me to an anti-racist person, anti-racist artist, philosopher, thinker, writer, and I had a list. And their first question was, "Who is going to see it?" I was like, "What do you mean who's going to see it? I'm going to see it. What are you talking about?" But there was this concern that if they created a video and it wasn't polished enough that it would follow them, or people would tease them or it would degrade somehow the brand of [HBCU] or their own personal brand. And I just find that just incredibly sad that our world is so outward facing. And as I say, thirsty for affirmation that we often will not attempt things that we are not sure we can excel at. Which is the opposite of the Christian life. Our work is to do the impossible. No, we don't have what it takes to make it happen and leave room for the holy spirit.

LEADING INDIVIDUALS TO THEOLOGICAL REFLECTION: "AND THERE WAS LIGHT"

Dean Hampton provided the awakening that is promised in Morehouse College motto "and there was light." He critiqued biblical literalists and the church. He noted how he addresses this issue with his students, giving them space to make reflection by saying:

People are always projecting negativity onto the transcendent level and it's partly because we believe in the devil as strongly as we believe in God. Not understanding that you can't have two ultimates in a universe. It's a universe, not a duoverse.

Reverend Waters' commentary was also directed to students and administrators and the idea of creating space for mistakes and a reflection on God's restoration. She disclosed:

So I had this motto, do your best and God will be praised, because if God is so, so fragile that if you proclaim the gospel wrong that our prayers don't get there, then that is not a God. That's not our God. I feel like I'm bringing that same spirit into my work at [HBCU],…That we have to be able to try. That we have to make an offering and leave room for the holy spirit to do what God will do with it. That we don't have to be perfect out of the gate because that's insanity and it will kill us. And it is a function of White supremacy that there's a standard that must be met by everyone else. So, I think that's my sermon for administrators. It is a school. Ain't that what you do at schools? You try new things, you learn from your failures, so that when you get out into the world you can say, I failed these ways, but maybe I'm going to try a new way.

DEFINING GENDER DYNAMICS: "KNOWLEDGE, LEADERSHIP, SERVICE"

In their own words, Black religious and spiritual life leaders at HBCUs discussed their power by defining gender dynamics. This is the Knowledge, Leadership, and Service mentioned in the motto of Tuskegee University.

Pastor Howard shared that when she had to challenge power as a woman not just from a racial perceptive but across denomination and religious affiliations:

> When you are working in a predominantly African American culture, there are practices and beliefs that come. And most of the time, if you're from the Black church, you think of male as the leader. And I've been in settings where I'm there with everyone else and they will talk to someone else to say, "Well, who's the director?" And they'll say, "Pastor [Howard]." "Oh." And you could see on their face where they have either thought of ... And I'm using this. Some don't believe women should lead in the capacity that I'm leading. And it's not just Christian, it's also Muslim, it's also Hindu. And I've been in those conversations. And what that has done for me is to be stronger in my identity as a person of color, but predominantly as a person of the gender that I'm in. But then the other side to that is, in the presence of our students, I have found many students to say, "Oh, I've never had a Black female pastor, or a woman pastor."

Dean Hampton, as a male, expressed his understanding of the power challenges that exist in gender. Through his narrative, he lifted an example and analyzed a woman who challenged perceived limitations. He detailed:

> I'm trying to remember when I first became aware of gender violence. In the Black Baptist church, I knew early that women did not have the same power and authority as the men, and what surprised me was that the women seemed to be comfortable with that arrangement and the men also. "I had an experience at one of the churches in...... I thought was just a terrible example of gender violence." I've seen this many times and it's where the men are sitting in the pulpit, the preachers, and it's time for the announcements, as was true in this instance that I'm reporting to you. The lady who got up from the pews in the congregation to approach the mic to make the announcements started coming up the steps into the pulpit. The pastor stood up and, pointing with an authoritarian gesture, pointing to a lectern on the floor, saying to her, "That is where you are supposed to speak and this is where we are supposed to speak, the clergy. That lectern is for you." His tone of voice and his gesture suggested that he was subordinating the woman. It's like saying that she was not worthy, like she was going to contaminate the pulpit, and it was disgusting. After the announcements, it came time for another part of the liturgy to be carried out in the service and a

woman was designated to do it. She walked up in the pulpit and she lectured the pastor that her father, who pastored before him, would have never insisted that women not enter the pulpit. She rubbed steel wool across his soul and it was uncomfortable for everybody. But everybody, I think, in the church was saying that the pastor had earned that.

Dr. Smith lived the very experience that Dean Hampton did. She pointed to a particular story and said:

And so, I can remember when my mother passed, going back home years later to take care of my grandmother. And my grandmother was not a fan of female preachers. The whole environment at home was not so. And so, I got called everything from the anti-Christ to all kinds of things. If I spoke, I spoke on the floor. If they were talking or conjugating, I had to wait outside. It was just a really rough scenario, as a Black female, trying to preach. And so, it's been a tough road, when I got here. I direct a ministers network. That truly was a good old boy network. And so, it got rough enough for me to even think about, maybe I need to do something else. But the Lord wouldn't let me, because this was an assignment I was called to and I couldn't just give it up, because I didn't place myself here.

Reverend Waters raised similar issues with being a woman as a religious and spiritual life leader. This situation led her to question her role. She said:

In HBCUs it's still I think a really tough nut to crack as a woman. In cabinet meetings, the assistant director… I mean, the athletic director is often asked to pray and I'm there. And I just say… I am in observation mode with that. Because I have two kinds of things running through my mind – Well, okay, they asked him to pray because he's a man, but then maybe they asked him to pray because he prays in the idiom and the tradition of Southern Baptist.

Dean Paine owned the privilege and power he had been afforded as a male. He attributed his classmates, both in seminary and in undergraduate college, as ones who helped him to acknowledge ways to reset. He mentioned using the privilege to embark upon hard conversations with his students, sharing vulnerable information about his life's own journey. He narrated:

I think we often talk about privilege in terms of White privilege and how various White people are not aware of their privilege and their access to power. They aren't aware of their microaggressions and sometimes aware of their aggressive behavior. I think I wasn't aware of my privilege as a male in the Black church. And my privilege was brought to my attention by my sisters at [HBCU], I thank God for them, my sisters at [PWI], and my sisters in the

African Methodist Episcopal Church. By analogy, I think that the attrition of Black women in the church is largely a byproduct of the sexist, the misogynistic, the heteronormative behavior that goes unchecked in our congregations. And the problem with that is that it seeks to minimize and limit God's gifts as expressed through these remarkable women, and they have to overcome these barriers to success in order to become fully human, i.e., realize their divine potential.

Pastor Howard used her power in ways that were unconventional. Through meekness and modesty, she's led from behind, using her power to elevate marginalized and oppressed groups. She described:

> The word that comes to mind is humility and humbleness, and then sacrifice. I can remember many, many different settings that I've been in where I didn't wear a collar. I didn't wear a collar intentionally. I didn't sit at the front. I didn't want to be recognized as the first connection that they had with me a clergy. I wanted them to know that, first of all, I'm Black like you, or second of all, mom, I'm a mother too. I recognize that there's a power that comes with that, but I've taken the back seat, I've humbled myself and let my transgender student speak. I have tried to say, "My power, you don't receive. And I don't have to exercise that in this setting, so let me let my transgender students speak to you, because I know you don't welcome them. Let me let my female other students speak to you because I know you don't welcome them." You've got to learn to be comfortable in conflict. You've got to learn to be able to deal with those that are your opposition, or those that don't agree because you are a certain color, because you are a certain gender, or because of how you are, your personality. But make true that you're okay with that. Make true you are strong in that first of all, and then you can handle the opposition.

Dr. Fisk used the power of preaching to heal and defy normalized patriarchy on his campus and in the pulpit. He explained:

> I'm cognizant that I don't use power as a bludgeon. I think that's probably the most important thing for me is that I've never wanted the pulpit or the teaching space to be used as a bludgeon against people in their fears And of course, I grew up in the time when women were just told to stay in their place. In fact, women weren't even allowed to preach when I was coming up, though I knew many women preachers. They called them missionaries back then. They wouldn't call them ministers or preachers, but they preached when they got up. There is no power, but God's. I am not a power broker. I don't want to be a power broker. I want to be a healer.

To summarize, Black religious and spiritual life leaders considered their purpose to be a combination of advocacy, pastoral care, institutional support, and leading individuals to theological reflection. They also defined gender dynamics in their roles. They were forthright in sharing in how they are redefining or reclaiming their role on the campus, either as a critique or to advance beyond their current state.

POWER

All ten participants mentioned the church broadly and the Black church specifically as an influencing and supporting component of their Black identity. From desiring to be in the church and part of church leadership to participants calling themselves "a result of the Black church," there were various success stories credited to the church. While participants' love for the Black church was adamant and resolute, some participants, in their love of the church, were not afraid to criticize it through accounts of abuse and mishandling. Additionally, dealings with predominately White church denominations affected some of the participants' Black identity.

H. Patrick Swygert, a past president of Howard University, wrote "that there is a special kind of nurturing that is only found in Black colleges: nurturing that daily enforces the notion of achievement and excellence."[35] The participants in this study described reports of significant exchanges at HBCUs. Participants recognized HBCUs as the place that gave them the means to be effective leaders and the space to be fostered on daily basis, not just during times of college-tour visits or parents weekends, as a show. These accounts complement Swygert's reflection and extend the earlier observations that the spaces of HBCUs morphed into safe havens for Black students and subsequent leaders.

Beyond the physical buildings where Black religious and spiritual life leaders served (including historic chapels and memorial chapels), advocacy, interestingly, was not just for Black students but for all. The participants spoke of the need to share the importance of advocating for people of color, religious minorities, and LGBTQ+ student populations. Participants widened this thought by sharing that they are called upon not just to help, but to lead campus communities in times of tragedy, misfortune, and calamity. In many instances, the religious and spiritual life leader is the first to be called in situations of catastrophe.

The participants, all ten of whom hold Master of Divinity degrees, chronicled historical moments in seminary that prompted a meaningful response to the awareness of Black identity as well as identity reframed from a gender perspective with theological implications. Participants also shared how their Black identity was restructured in thought while in seminary. (Davis et al. discussed the ideas of pluralism, peer-to-peer work, and how the work of diversity and religion was implemented and shared through religious and spiritual life.)[36] Some study participants described how their ideas about interfaith work and theological concepts were formulated from seminary and divinity school encounters. The participants' attribution of these changes to seminary and divinity school increases the need for further discussion in terms of the role of such institutions within the field religious and spiritual life. The Black religious and spiritual life leaders who participated in this study did not feel that their role was just one they "fell into" or happened to embark upon. Instead, they chronicled instances of calling.

In closing, I share an experience with a Black religious and spiritual life leader who was able to demonstrate past, purpose and power in one instance: Dean Bernard L. Richardson, a Black religious and spiritual life leader and a follower of Howard Thurman, known for his soul-stirring prayers, *once prayed for me.* One Saturday night in October 2015, I was out of the country at a conference in the Bahamas when I received a FaceTime call from an unknown number. Because I did not know the number, I did not pick up the call. The number called me back and out of curiosity and concern I picked up. I quickly realized that I was viewing the bricks of my brother's residence hall as the lights of what appeared to be an ambulance were being reflected. I immediately recognized the person FaceTiming me as the graduate director of my brother's Howard University residence hall. I am sure I looked frantic, bracing myself for news I never wanted to hear. He quickly began to reassure me that everything was okay. He informed me that my brother had suffered what appeared to be multiple seizures. This was particularly alarming and peculiar, as my brother had never suffered such medical issues. Within two hours, I boarded a flight back to Washington, D.C., in order to care for him. We spent the night at the Howard University Hospital. He slept as I paced the floor, crying and keeping my parents, who were thousands of miles away, informed of his condition. I awakened early the next morning to two distinct encounters. The first was a phone call from the associate dean of the chapel at Howard University, Kanika Magee Jones. She contacted me and prayed for my brother and me and inquired about his welfare. Moments later the dean of the chapel walked into the hospital room. This was significant because it was the university's International Sunday, one of the chapel's largest Sundays of the academic year. Instead of worrying about meeting the acclaimed international speaker, welcoming the thousands of parishioners who were preparing to worship in Cramton Auditorium, or thinking of the million people who would listen in on the radio, this Black religious and spiritual life leader was at the bedside of my brother, literally laying his hand on my brother's head and praying for him – and also praying for me. Talk about "Truth and Service"! I was later told by the doctor that Dean Richardson had spoken to him and instructed him to give my brother the very best care. I was awestricken.

The old Baptist hymn of my childhood, "A Charge to Keep I Have," written by Methodist leader Charles Wesley embodied my experience with a Black religious and spiritual life leader—a leader keeping the charge taken; serving this present age, fulfilling the call of duty; doing God's will; walking in the tradition of the past; operating in his gift and purpose which was the use of prayer; and wielding his power as university administrator.

NOTES

1. Albert A. Goodson, "We've Come This Far by Faith." (1956) (Manna Music Inc., 1963).
2. J. John Thelin, *A History of American Higher Education* (Baltimore, MD: JHU Press, 2011).
3. An important note is that qualitative inquiry cannot and should not be generalized broadly. Though quantitative inquiry lends itself to causality, the purpose and intent of this qualitative inquiry was not to generalize Black religious and spiritual life leaders. In order to make meaning, qualitative inquiry seeks rich, deep understanding. Future research could take a quantitative approach with a larger sample, with focus on predictability.
4. Rebecca Barton, Wendy Cadge, and Elena van Stee, "Caring for the Whole Student: How Do Chaplains Contribute to Campus Life?" *Journal of College and Character* 21, no. 2 (2020): 67–85; Sabin P. Landry, Jr., "Christian Ministry to the Campus in Historical Perspective," *Review & Expositor* 69, no. 3 (1972): 311–21.
5. Barton, Cadge, van Stee, "Caring for the Whole Student."
6. Landry, Jr., "Christian Ministry to the Campus in Historical Perspective."
7. John Schmalzbauer, "Campus Religious Life in America: Revitalization and Renewal," *Society* 50, no. 2 (2013): 115–31; Alexander W. Astin, Helen S. Astin, and Jennifer A. Lindholm, *Cultivating the Spirit: How College Can Enhance Students' Inner Lives* (New York: John Wiley & Sons, 2010); Alyssa Bryant Rockenbach, and Matthew J. Mayhew, "The Campus Spiritual Climate: Predictors of Satisfaction Among Students With Diverse Worldviews," *Journal of College Student Development* 55, no. 1 (2014): 41–62.
8. M. Meyers, "In the Name of God: A Survey of the Ritual, Intellectual, and Spiritual Manifestations of Religions on Campus." *The Pennsylvania Gazette* (1986).
9. James D. Anderson, *The Education of Blacks in the South, 1860-1935* (Chapel Hill: University of North Carolina Press, 1988).
10. Julien B. Roebuck, and Komanduri S. Murty, *Historically Black Colleges and Universities: Their Place in American Higher Education* (Westport, CT: Praeger Publishers, 1993).
11. Joseph N. Evans, *Lifting the Veil Over Eurocentrism: The Du Boisian Hermeneutic of Double Consciousness* (Trenton, NJ: Africa World Press, 2014).
12. James D. Anderson, *The Education of Blacks in the South, 1860-1935* (Chapel Hill: University of North Carolina Press, 1988).
13. Ibid.

14. Roebuck and Murty, *Historically Black Colleges and Universities*; Rayford W. Logan, *Howard University: The First Hundred Years 1867-1967* (New York: New York University Press, 1969); Addie Louise Joyner Butler, *The Distinctive Black College – Talladega, Tuskegee, and Morehouse* (Metuchen, NJ; London: The Scarecrow Press, Inc., 1977).

15. Anderson, *Education of Blacks in the South.*

16. Florence M. Read, *The Story of Spelman College* (Atlanta, GA: Spelman College, 1961): 299–300.

17. Logan, *Howard University.*

18. Conrad Cherry, Betty A. DeBerg, and Amanda Porterfield, *Religion on Campus* (Chapel Hill: University of North Carolina Press, 2001); Rebecca Barton, *Religion on Campus: Focus on Chaplains* (Brandeis University, 2018).

19. Cherry, Deberg, and Porterfield, *Religion on Campus.*

20. Morehouse College.

21. Howard University.

22. Miranda Threlfall-Holmes, and Mark Newitt, *Being a Chaplain* (New York: SPCK Library of Ministry, 2011).

23. Barton, Cadge, and van Stee, "Caring for the Whole Student"; Janice K. Davis. Merrily S. Dunn, and J. Shay Davis, "In Their Own Words: Campus Ministers' Perceptions of Their Work and Their Worlds," *College Student Affairs Journal* 23, no. 2 (2004): 173–84; Frederick T. Faison, "The Role and Relevance of the Historically Black College and University Chaplain," Doctoral diss., Union Institute and University, 2017; Lucy A. Forster-Smith, ed., *College & University Chaplaincy in the 21st Century: A Multifaith Look at the Practice of Ministry on Campuses Across America* (Nashville, TN: SkyLight Paths Publishing, 2013); Phillip E. Hammond, *The Campus Clergyman* (New York: Basic Books, 1964).

24. Parker Rossman, "The Morale of the Campus Pastor," *Religious Education* 57, no. 2 (1962): 110–160.

25. Hammond, *The Campus Clergyman*, 1964.

26. Jeffrey K. Hadden, *The Campus Clergyman* (New York: Basic Books, 1968).

27. Ernest Gordon, *Meet Me at the Door* (New York: Harper & Row, 1969).

28. Davis, Dunn, and Davis, "In Their Own Words."

29. John Schmalzbauer, "Campus Prophets, Spiritual Guides, or Interfaith Traffic Directors? The Many Lives of College and University Chaplains." *The Luce Lectures on the Changing Role of Chaplains in American Higher Education*, 2018.

30. Barton, Cadge, and van Stee, "Caring for the Whole Student."

31. Mark S. Giles, "Howard Thurman, Black Spirituality, and Critical Race Theory in Higher Education," *The Journal of Negro Education* 79 (2010): 354–65.

32. Frederick Rudolph, *The American College and University: A History* (Athens: University of Georgia Press, 1990).

33. Forster-Smith, *College & University Chaplaincy in the 21st Century.*

34. Faison, *The Role and Relevance of the Historically Black College and University Chaplain.*

35. Haywood Patrick Swygert, "The Constitution and Commitment to Black Access to Higher Education," *The Howard Law Journal* 30, no. 4 (1987): 1118.

36. Davis, Dunn, and Davis, "In Their Own Words: Campus Ministers' Perceptions of Their Work and Their Worlds."

REFERENCES

Anderson, James D. *The Education of Blacks in the South, 1860-1935.* Chapel Hill: University of North Carolina Press, 1988.

Astin, Alexander W., Astin, Helen S., and Lindholm, Jennifer A. *Cultivating the Spirit: How College Can Enhance Students' Inner Lives.* New York: John Wiley & Sons, 2010.

Barton, Rebecca, Cadge, Wendy, and van Stee, Elena. "Caring for the Whole Student: How Do Chaplains Contribute to Campus Life?" *Journal of College and Character* 21, no. 2 (2020): 67–85.

Butler, Addie Louise Joyner. *The Distinctive Black College – Talladega, Tuskegee, and Morehouse.* Metuchen, NJ; London: The Scarecrow Press, Inc., 1977.

Cherry, Conrad, DeBerg, Betty A., and Porterfield, Amanda. *Religion on Campus.* Chapel Hill: University of North Carolina Press, 2001.

Davis, Janice K., Dunn, Merrily S., and Davis, J. Shay. "In Their Own Words: Campus Ministers' Perceptions of Their Work and Their Worlds." *College Student Affairs Journal* 23, no. 2 (2004): 173–84.

Evans, Joseph N. *Lifting the Veil Over Eurocentrism: The Du Boisian Hermeneutic of Double Consciousness.* Trenton, NJ: Africa World Press, 2014.

Faison, Frederick T. "The Role and Relevance of the Historically Black College and University Chaplain," Doctoral diss., Union Institute and University, 2017.

Giles, Mark S. "Howard Thurman, Black Spirituality, and Critical Race Theory in Higher Education." *The Journal of Negro Education* 79 (2010): 354–65.

Goodson, Albert A. "We've Come This Far by Faith," words and music, 1956, Manna Music Inc., 1963.

Gordon, Ernest. *Meet Me at the Door.* New York: Harper & Row, 1969.

Landry, Sabin P. Jr. "Christian Ministry to the Campus in Historical Perspective." *Review & Expositor* 69, no. 3 (1972): 311–21.

Logan, Rayford W. *Howard University: The First Hundred Years 1867-1967.* New York: New York University Press, 1969.

Lucy A. Forster-Smith, ed., *College & University Chaplaincy in the 21st Century: A Multifaith Look at the Practice of Ministry on Campuses Across America.* Nashville, TN: SkyLight Paths Publishing, 2013.

McKittrick, Katherine. "On Plantations, Prisons, and a Black Sense of Placex." *Social & Cultural Geography* 12, no. 8 (2011): 947–63.

Meyers, M. "In the Name of God: A Survey of the Ritual, Intellectual, and Spiritual Manifestations of Religions on Campus." *The Pennsylvania Gazette,* 1986.

Mustaffa, Jalil Bishop. "Mapping Violence, Naming Life: A History of Anti-Black Oppression in the Higher Education System." *International Journal of Qualitative Studies in Education* 30, no. 8 (2017): 711–27.

Read, Florence M. *The Story of Spelman College.* Atlanta, GA: Spelman College, 1961.

Rockenbach, Alyssa Bryant, and Mayhew, Matthew J. "The Campus Spiritual Climate: Predictors of Satisfaction Among Students with Diverse Worldviews." *Journal of College Student Development* 55, no. 1 (2014): 41–62.

Roebuck, Julien B., and Murty, Komanduri S. *Historically Black Colleges and Universities: Their Place in American Higher Education.* Westport, CT: Praeger Publishers, 1993.

Rossman, Parker. "The Morale of the Campus Pastor." *Religious Education* 57, no. 2 (1962): 110–60.

Rudolph, Frederick. *The American College and University: A History.* Athens: University of Georgia Press, 1990.

Schmalzbauer, John. "Campus Religious Life in America: Revitalization and Renewal." *Society* 50, no. 2 (2013): 115–31.

Schmalzbauer, John. "Campus Prophets, Spiritual Guides, or Interfaith Traffic Directors? The Many Lives of College and University Chaplains." *The Luce Lectures on the Changing Role of Chaplains in American Higher Education*, 2018. https://www.tandfonline.com/doi/full/10.1080/2194587X.2021.1898984

Schmalzbauer, John, and Mahoney, Kathleen A. *The Resilience of Religion in American Higher Education.* Waco, TX: Baylor University Press, 2018.

Schmalzbauer, John, Waggoner, Michael D., and Walker, Nathan C. "Campus Ministry." In *The Oxford Handbook of Religion and American Education*, edited by Michael D. Waggoner, and Nathan C. Walker, 453–66. Oxford: Oxford University Press, 2018.

Swygert, Haywood Patrick. "The Constitution and Commitment to Black Access to Higher Education." *The Howard Law Journal* 30, no. 4 (1987): 1109–19.

www.ingramcontent.com/pod-product-compliance
Lightning Source LLC
Chambersburg PA
CBHW070350270326
41926CB00017B/4066